HAWAIIAN RAILWAY

VOLUME 2 - ALONG THE MAIN LINES OF
THE OAHU RAILWAY & LAND CO. AND
THE HAWAII CONSOLIDATED RAILWAY

WWII PHOTOGRAPHS BY VICTOR NORTON, JR.

WRITTEN BY GALE E. TREIBER

To Victor Norton...

And the several other World War II servicemen
who photographed and preserved railroad scenes in Hawaii
so that we can enjoy them today.

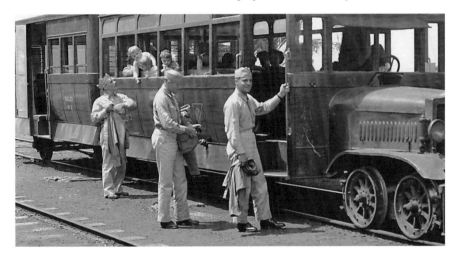

Printed with pride
in the U.S.A.

Front Cover: A passenger extra from Barbers Point approaches Waipahu on its way to Honolulu. This two-track bridge, still standing today, crosses Kapakahi Stream just west of the station site. The semaphore signal to the right of #88's smokebox marks the entrance to the Wahiawa Branch, which curves off to the right.

Rear Cover Top: Servicemen disembark for an unexpected photo opportunity along the Hawaii Consolidated Railway's Hamakua Division as railbus #3 waits for a local freight to clear the main line.

The Railroad Press
PO Box 444
Hanover, PA 17331-0444

Printed in the United States of America.

International Standard Book Number 1-931477-14-0

Publishers of:

TRP Magazine

PRR Lines West Pittsburgh to St. Louis 1960-1999

Illinois Central: North of the Ohio River

ALCO's to Allentown

Altoona Action

Passenger Cars of New England

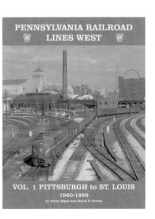

INTRODUCTION

ABOVE: Number 80, a 2-8-2 built by Alco Schenectady in 1926, backs through OR&L's main yard at Iwilei. The engine servicing facility and roundhouse are directly behind #80's tender. These 36" gauge locomotives were patterned after D&RGW's successful K28 class and weighed 78 tons -- quite a large size for an American narrow gauge locomotive.

Volume 1 of this Hawaiian Railway Album series introduced Victor Norton, an amateur rail photographer who was stationed at the Ship Repair Unit of Navy Yard Pearl Harbor during the latter stages of World War II. That volume presented photographs of the Oahu Railway and Land Company taken in the vicinity of that railroad's passenger station, roundhouse and yard in the Iwilei section of Honolulu. Victor's high resolution photographs show in great detail the railroad action there during the War.

This volume shows Victor's scenes taken along the Oahu Railway's main line that extended some seventy miles from downtown Honolulu to Kahuku on Oahu's North Shore. After leaving Honolulu the line passed Pearl Harbor and continued to the junction at Waipahu where OR&L's major branch line, to the pineapple fields in the center of the island, left the main line. From Waipahu the main line continued westward through seemingly endless sugar cane fields until it reached Oahu's rugged Leeward Coast. There the line turned in a northerly direction and followed the coast through Waianae and beyond, along the most scenic portion of the line, until it reached Kaena Point where it turned eastward toward the sugar mill town of Waialua. Beyond Waialua, the main line passed through Haleiwa and skirted beautiful Waimea Bay on the way to its terminus at another sugar mill town, Kahuku.

At the outset of World War II, rail passenger service had almost been eliminated, with OR&L buses taking over all regularly scheduled passenger service except the rail-motorcar commuter runs between Honolulu and Ewa. Before the War occasional excursions had been run from Honolulu to the North Shore town of Haleiwa for tourists, but these ended with the attack on Pearl Harbor. Victor made numerous trips to downtown Honolulu to photograph trains in Iwilei, always well within the confines of railroad property, since wartime restrictions throughout the islands prevented photography anywhere that might be considered as a restricted or militarily sensitive area. For this reason Victor did not take pictures out along the main line until after the end of the War, when photography restrictions were lifted. As soon as he could he hitchhiked from Pearl Harbor to Waipahu, to photograph OR&L operations at the junction for the Wahiawa Branch, as well as the nearby sugar plantation railway owned by the Oahu Sugar Company. As you will see, he did a nice job documenting that trip for us.

Then in December of 1945, the OR&L resumed excursion operations on their main line from Honolulu to Haleiwa. The train stopped along the way for water at both Waipahu and Waianae, and then made a photo stop at one of the most scenic points along the rugged coast, Arch Rock, just south of Kaena Point. Victor rode this trip and once again provided some beautiful pictures for us.

In addition to the above photos, I have included several more views of the OR&L in Honolulu that would not fit in the first volume. Once again the OR&L photos are laid out in a geographic sequence, from Honolulu to Haleiwa, which is far as Victor traveled along the OR&L main line.

Victor said that toward the end of the War, the barracks rumor mill indicated that those sailors who did not use their annual allocation of ten days shore leave would be permitted to muster out of the Navy earlier than those that did. That rumor was not true, and fortunately for us Victor did not believe it and spent his leave in 1945 and 1946 visiting and photographing trains on the Big Island and Kauai respectively. The second half of this book shows most of the views of the Hawaii Consolidated Railway that Victor took during his trip to the island of Hawaii (the "Big Island") in May of 1945. During his time on the Big Island he walked from Hilo to HCR's roundhouse and yard at Waiakea, and then he rode the regularly scheduled HCR railbus from Hilo to Paauilo on the Hamakua (northern) Division. As you will see, this stretch of railroad was one of the most spectacular in the world!

Believing that many readers will buy all three volumes of the Hawaiian Railway Album, I have decided not to repeat the OR&L history from the first book. However, to balance the obviously needed history for the Hawaii Consolidated Railway, I have elected to provide a historical description of the OR&L main line, and I have included segments of the company's official map from 1943. In addition I have included copies of OR&L and HCR fare receipts -- showing all of the stops along their main lines -- plus tickets from Victor's collection and timetables from various sources. I hope these will be helpful to the reader in understanding how these systems operated.

As you read this book, please remember that it takes more than great photographs and insightful captions to make a successful book. At this time I would like to thank the Hawaiian Railway Society for backing this project, and their Historian Emeritus, Bob Paoa -- undoubtedly the world's expert on Hawaii's railway history -- who spends a lot of time reviewing these volumes and then correcting my errors and providing information about obscure background details. Thanks are also due to Big Island railway historians Ian Birnie, John May and Neil Erickson, for providing valuable information about the Hawaii Consolidated Railway, to my son, John Treiber, who prepared the maps for this volume and to Gordon Ng, from Colorprints in Honolulu, who continues to works magic with Victor's negatives, removing flaws and bringing out details in the prints used in this book, taking them from very good to excellent. Next I would like to thank TRP's Jaime Serensits for his faith and guidance in developing this three-book project. And again I want to thank Victor Norton for both taking these wonderful photographs, and then donating his Hawaiian railway negatives to the Hawaiian Railway Society so that they could be shared with railroad enthusiasts around the world through these volumes. Finally, there is a special thanks due to my wife, Georgia, for her encouragement, as well as her patience, as I work alone in my computer room putting these books together. So, a hearty thanks to all of you!

Gale E. Treiber
Kapolei, Hawaii
July 2004

OAHU RAILWAY AND LAND COMPANY

ABOVE: 4-6-0 #64 sits in the afternoon sun, ready to depart for Barbers Point Naval Air Station. It will return with another trainload of sailors headed for an evening of liberty. From Honolulu station, they will more than likely walk to nearby "downtown" or ride the trolley-bus to Waikiki. The little locomotive was built by the Baldwin Locomotive Works in 1898 and weighed only 30 tons, but she was still quite active hauling passenger extras (note the white flags) during the War.

The Oahu Railway and Land Company, Ltd., the third common carrier railroad in the Kingdom of Hawaii, was founded by Benjamin Franklin Dillingham in 1889. Whether one might call it good fortune or bad, young Frank Dillingham, then an American merchant sailor, was left behind in the Kingdom of Hawaii in 1865 to recuperate from a broken leg suffered while returning from a horseback ride in the hills of Oahu. During his extended stay in Hawaii he fell in love with the islands and spent the rest of his life in residence there. He struggled financially for most of his early career, but he eventually became a respected and successful businessman.

One of Mr. Dillingham's dreams was to lease some land for development in the vast, desolate Ewa coral plain on the southwest corner of his home island of

Oahu. That part of Oahu is in the "rain shadow" of the Koolau Mountains, so little could be grown there without an external source of water. However, once James Campbell dug Hawaii's first successful artesian well on his land in Honouliuli, just west of what is today called Pearl Harbor, tapping into the huge aquifer under the island, the region's water problem was resolved and Mr. Dillingham's plans could proceed.

Although crops could then be grown and people survive on the Ewa coral plain, another problem became apparent -- the lack of reliable transportation between that area and Oahu's principal port, Honolulu. Frank Dillingham had ridden railways in other areas of the would, and in fact was quite familiar with the railways just starting to be built in the Kingdom of Hawaii, so he proposed a railway line from Honolulu to the Pearl River Lagoon (Pearl Harbor). On September 11, 1888, after a great deal of political maneuvering by Mr. Dillingham, King Kalakaua signed a railway bill granting him the exclusive rights and the power of eminent domain to build a railroad line from Honolulu to Manana (which would eventually become the town of Pearl City), some fifteen miles away, on the northern side of Pearl Harbor. From the outset Mr. Dillingham decided that the line should use the narrow gauge of 36" between the rails to save construction costs. He then began the difficult task of raising funds locally, brought in an experienced engineer to survey and lay out the railway line, ordered construction equipment, purchased land for the right-of-way and commenced construction. He chartered his railroad as the Oahu Railway and Land Company, Limited, ordered locomotives, cars and rail and eventually commenced operations between Honolulu and Halawa, very close to today's Aloha Stadium, on the King's birthday, the 16th of October, in 1889.

Opening with neither a large source of freight nor passenger traffic in the villages along the line, local skeptics were sure the enterprise would soon fail. However, Frank Dillingham persisted, and his little

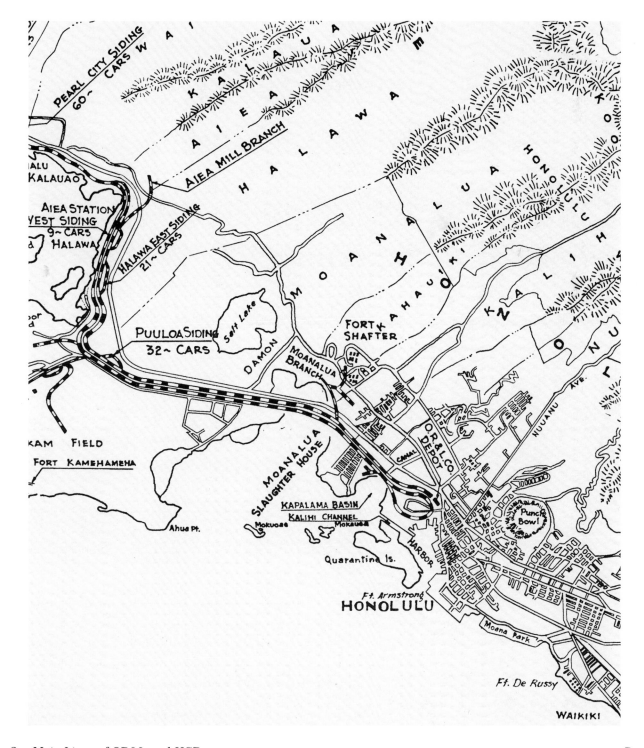

Hawaiian Railway Album

OPPOSITE ABOVE: OR&L #31, a Baldwin 2-8-0, prepares to leave Honolulu Station with a 13-car train. The notes in Victor's photo album indicates that this is a "Pearl Harbor train." As Oahu's roads improved and passengers deserted the railway in the 1930's, many of the line's passenger and baggage cars were considered excess and were converted to shuttle cans between the local manufacturer and the pineapple canneries. However, once WWII began, they were quickly reconverted by adding benches and stanchions for standees. Glass windows were eventually reinstalled, but until that happened, it must have been a very warm ride for the shipyard commuters that crammed into these cars at the end of their shift for their 15-minute ride to downtown Honolulu.

OPPOSITE BELOW: Another shipyard train prepares to depart Honolulu. Locomotives running in reverse were the normal configuration for Pearl Harbor trains. There was no turning facility at the Navy Base, so locomotives ran around their trains and were then headed in the direction of Honolulu. Running forward presumably gave shipyard commuters and Fleet Landing liberty parties a faster trip to Honolulu. Number 98 was a 2-8-0 built by Baldwin in 1898. The large headlight on the tender illuminated the tracks while backing during night operations.

ABOVE: Five OR&L locomotives sit in the sunshine at Iwilei roundhouse on a quiet Sunday morning after the War ended. From left to right are GE 47-ton diesel-electric #19, Baldwin 4-6-0 #64, Alco 0-6-0 #12, Alco 2-8-0 #37 and Baldwin 2-8-0 #31. OR&L was one of the few U.S. narrow gauge railroads to use 0-6-0 switchers, and #12 remained in service even after the main line was abandoned at the end of 1947. It survives as a static display at the Hawaiian Railway Museum in Ewa. Number 19 survives as well, but at the Cumbres and Toltec Railroad in Chama, New Mexico.

railroad reached its authorized terminus of Manana by the first of January 1890. In November of 1889, he had finally concluded his transaction to lease James Campbell's 60,000 acres of ranchland on the Ewa plain. Mr. Dillingham then sub-leased that land to the Ewa Plantation Company, the first of several sugar plantations that would ensure a traffic base for his railroad. Next he worked through the legislature another bill to extend his railway line through Ewa to the west coast of Oahu and then north to the sugar town of Waianae, and also from Honolulu eastward, past Koko Head and up the eastern coast all the way to Kahuku.

BELOW: 4-6-0 #85 rests at OR&L's Iwilei steam locomotive servicing facility between passenger runs. Here locomotives replenished their supplies of heavy fuel oil, water for steam and sand for traction. The roundhouse and turntable sit directly behind #85's tender. This locomotive is another OR&L survivor, although it is now sitting in pieces, partially restored, at the Lahaina, Kaanapali & Pacific Railroad shops on the island of Maui.

OPPOSITE ABOVE: Here is another view of the Iwilei serving facility. Completely serviced and ready for outbound trains are, from left to right, 2-8-2 #80, 4-6-0 #85 and 2-8-0 #22. Number 80 was always easy to pick out from her sisters, once her smokebox cover was destroyed in a wreck and the OR&L shop force made the substitute from flat plate that you see in this photograph.

OPPOSITE BELOW: This is one of Victor's early OR&L photographs, taken in late 1943 or early 1944, before his parents sent him his large format camera. The locomotive shown is 2-8-0 #76, almost fifty years old, but still sparkling in the bright Hawaii sunshine. The locomotive still has a "blackout" cover on its headlight, to allow a little light to shine on the track ahead, but still minimize the amount that could be seen by hostile ships or submarines off the coast. Of perhaps even more interest are the buildings in the background, owned by Hawaiian Gas Products ("Gas Pro") and the canneries. Note Dole's pineapple-shaped water tower on the far right.

The former line was eventually built, while the latter never went beyond the survey stage. With this authorization, the OR&L reached its new terminus at the sugar town of Ewa in late 1890. In addition to this mainline extension, Mr. Dillingham ran a branch line from Pearl City southward through the Pearl City Peninsula to serve purchasers of large country lots there -- advertised as within easy railroad commuting distance from Honolulu -- that he was selling from the Land Company portion of the OR&L.

Historic events plagued the early railroad. First, in 1890, the McKinley Tariff Act rescinded the Reciprocity Treaty of 1876, and a tariff was once again placed on Hawaiian sugar entering the United States. Demand for Hawaiian sugar decreased, production dropped and rail traffic from the Ewa Plantation

ABOVE: Sisters #35 and #32 lead a morning westbound freight train for the Wahiawa Branch through Iwilei yard. These 2-8-0's were built in 1916 and 1913 respectively, and weighed a little over 50 tons each. Both outlasted the Oahu Railway, surviving until roughly 1975 on the Ferrocarril de El Salvador. Note the train crew, riding in the first boxcar and on the roof of the second. This was common practice for the OR&L, which for the most part had eliminated the use of cabooses long before the start of the War. That first boxcar was reportedly used for LCL freight, and appears to have benches and yellow doors.

dropped as well. In January of 1891 King Kalakaua died, and his sister, Princess Liliuokalani, ascended to the throne. In January 1893, when Queen Liliuokalani tried to promulgate a new constitution strengthening the powers of the Hawaiian Monarchy, the local business leaders who had long sought closer ties -- even annexation -- to the United States fomented a revolution and the Kingdom of Hawaii came to a close. The instability that resulted from these three events caused a turndown in the Hawaiian economy and losses for the OR&L, and this resulted in Mr. Dillingham being unable to raise either foreign or local capital to extend his railroad line. It was not until 1894 that construction on the line from Ewa to Waianae resumed. The year 1894 also brought the end to the U.S. tariffs on Hawaiian Sugar and found Mr. Dillingham developing another sugar plantation, the Oahu Sugar Company,

with its mill to be built in Waipahu, just off the main line between Pearl City and Ewa. The sugar traffic from this plantation, one of the most successful in Hawaii, finally put the Oahu Railway -- and Frank Dillingham -- on a firm financial footing.

The OR&L reached Waianae in 1895, and then construction continued in a northerly direction along the rugged Leeward Coast of Oahu to Kaena Point. Where the relatively flat land along the coast finally disappeared, a shelf just wide enough for a single track was blasted out of the lava cliffs about thirty feet above the sea, where furious Pacific Ocean waves would break during certain times of the year. This was undoubtedly the most scenic portion of the Oahu Railway, and it provided a wonderful ride for excursionists. After reaching rugged Kaena Point, the western-most point on Oahu, the line turned eastward and traveled first through desolate lava fields and eventually through the relatively flat plains west of the town of Waialua, where Frank Dillingham was already in the process of developing yet another sugar plantation, the Waialua Agricultural Company. Waialua was reached in June of 1898.

OR&L railway service reached the sugar town of Kahuku, just east of the northern tip of Oahu, on New Years Day, 1899. The main line of the Oahu Railway was finally complete, and with newly negotiated freight contracts in place with the Kahuku Plantation Company and the new Honolulu Plantation Company in Aiea, the OR&L then serviced six of the seven major sugar plantations on Oahu. Raw sugar from all of those mills -- plus refined sugar from Honolulu Plantation -- became the foundation for OR&L's freight traffic until the beginning of World War II.

With both incoming and outgoing traffic between the sugar plantations and Honolulu assured, Mr. Dillingham in 1901 purchased land adjacent to Honolulu Harbor, some above water and some below, that would soon be filled in, to resolve the shortage of rail accessible wharf and warehouse space at the harbor.

In 1905 Frank Dillingham decided to build OR&L's Wahiawa Branch. That line started at the end of the short spur that had previously been built north from the main line at Waipahu to service the Oahu Sugar Company's mill. The line was extended into Waikakalua Gulch and climbed some 900 feet in ten miles to reach the saddle between the Koolau and Waianae mountain ranges, the area where large-scale pineapple production had just begun. This was the most difficult climb on the OR&L, with 3% grades, a

ABOVE: Number 88, a 4-6-0 built by Alco in 1916, sits at the head of a passenger train at the west end of Iwilei Yard. On the left is OR&L's RIP ("Repair in Place") tracks and their car repair shop. An interesting selection of freight cars waits for repairs, including the U.S. Army boxcar on the far left. To the right of the train, one of the relatively new GE 47-ton diesel-electrics passes through the yard with the crew riding the footboards. Per Victor, OR&L's two diesels were usually used along Honolulu's waterfront.

COLORS OF THE OR&L DURING WORLD WAR II

After publication of the first volume of the Hawaiian Railway Album, I received several letters from modelers asking about the colors used by the railroad for its locomotives, cars and buildings. Color film was rare back then, and most serious rail photographers preferred their large format black and white images to 35mm color film. It is probably safe to say that there were very few color images taken of OR&L equipment prior to abandonment and the wholesale scrapping that followed. The Hawaiian Railway Society has only a small collection of OR&L color slides, and almost all of them are duplicates and therefore not sharp enough for publication. The Bishop Museum has the original 16mm film of OR&L's last passenger train from Kahuku to Honolulu on the 31st of December 1947, the last day for its main line operations. Based on these limited sources, we have assembled the following for the period at the end and right after World War II.

Steam Locomotives and Tenders: With the exception of the smokeboxes which were graphite gray, OR&L locomotives and tenders were all black, with white lettering, numbers and striping. (That said, the above mentioned movie has an overhead view of #70 which shows a dull red cab roof, which could have been rust but looks too uniform for that.) Wooden window frames were painted black, red, or light green. As a rule, smokebox number or star plates were polished brass with bright red paint as a background. (We have seen exceptions though. There is one color slide that shows #90's with brass letters and numbers on a black painted background, and there is a black and white movie scene showing #64's with a reversed scheme with black-painted lettering and numbers on a shiny brass background.) OR&L steam locomotive bells were brass, and after the War were almost always highly polished.

Diesel Locomotives: Numbers 15 and 19 were delivered in light gray with dark (presumably black) lettering. Before the end of the War they were repainted into the dark blue and silver scheme seen in Volume One.

Motor Cars: Before the War OR&L motorcars were painted silver and blue. In the early 1940's M1 and M2 were repainted into a dark green and silver scheme and remained that way until they were scrapped. M3 and M4 were pullman green during and after WWII.

Passenger Cars: These were painted pullman green, with black underbodies and trucks, flat black canvas roofs and white numbers and lettering. (The originally deep yellow second class and baggage cars had all been repainted into pullman green long before the War started.) It should be noted that in the 1947 movie mentioned above, three of the passenger cars in the train were painted coach green and they stood out from the more common pullman green cars which had by then faded to olive drab.

Freight Cars: OR&L's wooden cars were painted freight car red and their steel cars were painted black. As mentioned in the first volume, tank cars were often both colors, with the OR&L-owned wooden flatcar painted freight car red and the privately owned metal tank strapped to its deck painted black. All freight cars had black underbodies and trucks. The two cabooses were also believed to have been painted freight car red. Lettering was yellow on the red cars and white on the black cars.

Stations and Company Buildings: These were generally wood frame buildings, painted white with brown roofs. Honolulu Station, a concrete building, was pink, similar to today's Tripler Army hospital and Waikiki's Ala Moana Hotel. Station signs were made of wood and painted white with black lettering.

Service Facilities: The roundhouse at Iwilei was left in natural concrete, but parts of it were blackened by soot over the years. The corrugated metal roof on the second story addition for the heavy fuel tank on the west side of the roundhouse was painted dull red. The steam locomotive servicing bridge was black, as was the little sand car that rode on the rails along its top. The turntable was also black. Iwilei's wooden sand elevator and wooden water tank were both painted freight car red. Other water tanks along the line were painted either freight car red or pullman green.

General Note: Paints half a century ago did not have the UV protection found in today's paints, so they tended to fade quickly in Hawaii's intense tropical sunlight. They would be a dark shade of the colors described above when first applied, but then would soon fade to a much lighter shade. Also, color film hues tend to fade or shift as the film ages, and colors appear differently under changing lighting conditions. Making "exact" color matches from old images, without manufacturers' paint formulas or color chips, would be a real challenge.

BELOW: Another trainload of sailors from either Fleet Landing Pearl Harbor or Barbers Point Naval Air Station threads its way through the west end of Iwilei Yard, as the fireman watches track conditions on "his" side of the locomotive. The locomotive is 2-8-0 #31, and the first car in the train is doorless combine #48, which started life on the OR&L as B.F. Dillingham's first private observation car, "PEARL."

large "S" curve and many small, tight curves, so that double or triple-heading locomotives was normally required.

With the completion of the Wahiawa Branch in 1906, the OR&L had expanded as far as it would. Short branches were built to serve new industries and military bases along the main line as well as the Wahiawa Branch. None of these bases was so significant as the Army's new Schofield Barracks -- the largest Army base in the Pacific -- established on the Wahiawa Branch in 1907. This greatly expanded traffic on the Wahiawa Branch by adding a great deal of military traffic to its already booming pineapple business.

Dependable rail service and reasonable rates allowed the sugar and pineapple plantations to significantly increase their output, primarily by cultivating more and more land. Railway growth paralleled that of the agricultural industries it served, and the OR&L

received significant upgrades beginning in 1908. The main line was re-laid with heavier rail, bridges were strengthened and more powerful locomotives and hundreds of additional and larger freight cars were ordered. Honolulu's original wooden passenger station was enlarged in 1918 and then completely replaced with a concrete structure in 1925. In 1909 a new 15-stall concrete roundhouse and machine shop replaced the old wooden roundhouse in Iwilei, a short distance west of the Honolulu Station, where the railroad's passenger and freight yards were located. In 1913 the main line from Honolulu was rerouted to a slightly shorter, more level route along the shore from the Iwilei area to just past Salt Lake near the present day Honolulu International Airport, and the main line was completely double-tracked from Honolulu to Waipahu by 1921. Semaphore-type automatic block signals were installed from Honolulu to Waipahu

BELOW: Here is 4-6-0 #64, a product of the Baldwin Locomotive Works of Philadelphia that was delivered to the OR&L in 1898. The little Ten-wheeler had 43-inch diameter driving wheels and weighed only thirty tons, but still did her share during the busy War years. She is sitting on one of Iwilei's locomotive servicing tracks, with the open-air car repair shop in the background.

OPPOSITE ABOVE: This is the railroad portion of one of the OR&L's last passenger schedules, dated August 28, 1933. Although there was still a reasonable amount of local service between Honolulu and Ewa Mill, only one train remained on the 70-mile main line to Kahuku, and there was no longer rail passenger service on the Wahiawa Branch to the center of the island. Improved roads allowed this service to be handled by OR&L buses that went from Honolulu to Wahiawa, Schofield Barracks and then on to Haleiwa on the North Shore. Note the footnote regarding connecting rail motor car service between Haleiwa and Kahuku.

OPPOSITE BELOW: This is the busy junction at Waipahu, some 13 miles from Honolulu, where the Wahiawa Branch joined the main line. Victor visited Waipahu after the War ended and security restrictions had finally been lifted, and the following few photographs show us the results of his visit. This view looks east from the bridge over Kapakahi Stream. On the left is the passenger station, which also housed an operator who prepared train orders for both the main line and the branch. Note the train order board directly in front of the station, as well as the wig-wag, or banjo, warning signal for Depot Road that crossed the railway between the station and the bridge. There were three water tanks at Waipahu -- the one on the left for trains going up the Wahiawa Branch and the two on the right to serve the main line. In the distance a freight train waits for clearance to enter the Wahiawa Branch.

TRAINS TOWARD KAHUKU

STATIONS	Distance	17	3	27	9	11
		Daily A.M.	Daily A.M.	Daily A.M.	Daily P.M.	Daily P.M.
HONOLULU	0	8.00	9.15	11.00	3.00	5.15
PUULOA	6	8.12	9.30	11.12	3.13	5.27
F SUBMARINE	6	8.15	9.32	11.14	3.15	5.29
AIEA	8	8.20	9.37	11.20	3.22	5.35
PEARL CITY	11	‡ 8.28	‡ 9.46	‡11.28	‡ 3.32	‡ 5.45
WAIPAHU	13	8.34	9.52	11.34	3.38	5.53
HONOULIULI	15	8.40	10.00	11.42	3.45	6.00
EWA MILL	17	8.45	10.06	11.47	3.51	6.05
F NANAKULI	27		10.26			
WAIANAE	32		10.36			
F MAKUA	40		10.57			
F KAWAIHAPAI	49		11.18			
F MOKULEIA	51		11.22			
WAIALUA	55		11.31			
F HALEIWA	55		11.34			
F WAIMEA	61		11.46			
KAHUKU	70		12.06			

TRAINS TOWARD HONOLULU

STATIONS	Distance	18	4	26	6	12
		Daily A.M.	Daily A.M.	Daily A.M.	Daily P.M.	Daily P.M.
KAHUKU	0					2.02
F WAIMEA	10					2.22
F HALEIWA	15					2.34
WAIALUA	15					2.37
F MOKULEIA	19					2.46
F KAWAIHAPAI	21					2.50
F MAKUA	30					3.11
WAIANAE	38					3.27
F NANAKULI	44					3.40
EWA MILL	53	6.25	7.45	9.16	1.15	4.02
HONOULIULI	55	6.31	7.50	9.21	1.20	4.07
WAIPAHU	57	6.40	7.57	9.27	1.26	4.13
PEARL CITY	60	‡ 6.49	‡ 8.04	‡ 9.33	‡ 1.33	‡ 4.19
AIEA	62	7.00	8.13	9.41	1.41	4.27
F SUBMARINE	63	7.08	8.18	9.46	1.46	4.30
PUULOA	64	7.10	8.20	9.48	1.48	4.32
HONOLULU	70	7.27	8.32	10.00	2.00	4.45

A rail motor car will leave Kahuku at 6:00 A. M. daily, connecting with Bus No. 2 for Honolulu. After arrival of Bus No. 3 at Haleiwa, a rail motor car will leave for Kahuku.
F Flag Stops—Trains will also stop on signal at all regular Flag Stops.   ‡ Connections made with Peninsula Service.

where the branch to Wahiawa left the main line, then west beyond Waipahu to Honouliuli and north several miles up Waikakalua Gulch. Passenger service declined during the 1930's, with rail-motorcars and trailers taking over much of the traffic that remained. Excursion trains continued to run between Honolulu and OR&L's charming resort hotel in Haleiwa, so that tourist and local residents alike could still experience a journey along Oahu's rugged Leeward Coast.

Frank Dillingham had retired as general manager of the OR&L and turned its operation over to his son, Walter, in 1914. Walter continued to quite successfully guide the line in his father's tradition. In spite of a slight downturn in freight traffic during the Depression of the mid to late 1930s, the OR&L remained quite profitable. Reinvestment continued so that the railway's physical plant was in excellent condition, with sufficient capacity to absorb the massive amount of additional traffic soon to be brought by World War II. On line bases such as the Army's Fort Shafter, located on a branch from the original main line through Moanalua, the Kapalama Depot in Honolulu Harbor,

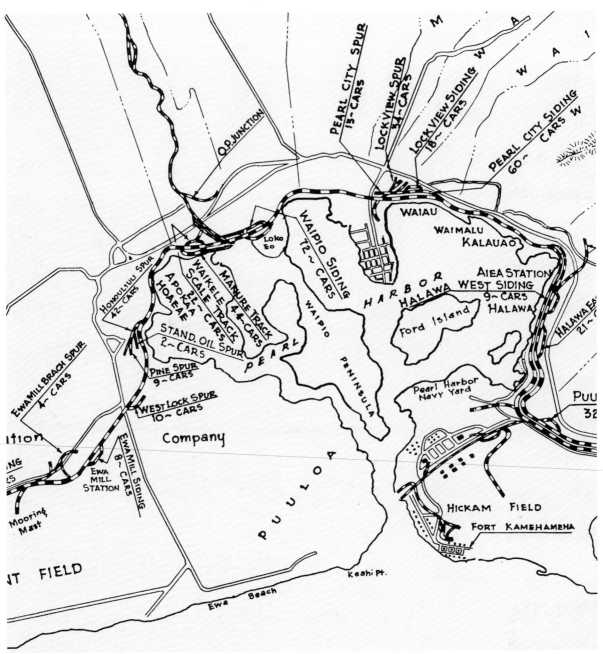

OPPOSITE ABOVE: A morning extra for Barbers Point with 4-6-0 #88 on the point halts for water at Waipahu. Scheduled passenger traffic through Waipahu had been reduced to railcar runs before the War, but driving restrictions, gas rationing and greatly increased traffic brought steam-hauled passenger trains back. This train will go into Barbers Point Naval Air Station and reverse directions there on a wye. Then it will return to Honolulu with another liberty party of Sailors and Marines.

OPPOSITE BELOW: Victor walked back to the rear of the empty train and watched while the crew took on water in the distance. Combine #37 is on the main line to Ewa, Waianae and Kahuku, and to its right sits the freight train we saw previously waiting in the distance, with a load of bombs headed for the Navy Ammunition Depot at Waikele, on the lower portion of the Wahiawa Branch.

Hickam Air Base on the main line east of Pearl Harbor, and Camp Kahuku at the end of the line, as well as Schofield Barracks and Wheeler Air Base on the Wahiawa Branch, plus the Navy's operating base, shipyard and ammunition loading facility at Pearl Harbor, its Naval Air Station at Barbers Point on the Ewa Plain and its Ammunition Depot at Lualualei on the Leeward Coast, plus many smaller facilities, together brought huge increases in passenger and freight traffic for the duration of the War, and the railway handled them -- along with its continuing agricultural traffic -- with apparent ease.

This then describes the OR&L as Hawaii was plunged into World War II. The physical plant was not much different when Victor Norton photographed it during the period 1943-1946. His photographs show a railroad thriving even under the strain of war. Passenger cars that had been converted to shuttle cans to the various pineapple canneries in the 1930s were hastily reconverted to passenger configuration and carried civilian War and Navy Department workers and other commuters between Honolulu and their worksites, as well as servicemen and women traveling between their bases and Honolulu for an evening of "liberty." Daily military charters were run from Honolulu to the Navy's Ammunition Depot at Lualualei, picking up civilian workers at stops along the way and then dropping them off at Hickam, Pearl Harbor, Barbers Point and Lualualei, where the train would lay over until its return trip to Honolulu. Only three locomotives were added to the Oahu Railway's roster during the War, but numerous freight and pas-

OPPOSITE: Number 44 above and #43 below, were OR&L's two Shay locomotives. They were purchased new from Lima in 1920 and 1921 respectively. Shays are interesting locomotives, with vertical cylinders driving a horizontal crankshaft that is connected to the locomotives trucks by a series of shafts and gears. OR&L's three-truck Shays had three cylinders, but unfortunately for us, they are on the other side of the locomotive, and the combination of the high weeds and sun angle prevented Victor from getting photographs of the other, more interesting, side. Shays were designed to be powerful and agile, but were somewhat slow. Purchased for use on the three percent grades of the Wahiawa Branch, these locomotives proved to be too slow for the OR&L, so they were set aside before the beginning of the War and sat on this siding in Waipahu until shortly before they were finally written off in 1948 and scrapped. The small 0-6-0T locomotive sitting off the end of the siding behind #43 in the photograph below is ex-Ruby Hill Railroad #1, which was built in 1875 and used by OR&L's sister firm, the Hawaiian Dredging Company.

ABOVE: Victor did not photograph the departure of the bomb train from Waipahu, but he did manage to catch 2-8-0 #32 on the rear, pushing the heavy train up the hill. Note the crew sitting on the bombs on the second flatcar in front of #32. The footbridge above #32 provided access to the Oahu Sugar Company's mill in Waipahu, which was located on the bluff to Victor's right. OSC's sugar cane cars can be seen in the upper right hand portion of this photograph.

ABOVE: Victor walked up along the Oahu Railway right-of-way, past the turnout that went back up the hill to the sugar mill, until he reached the point where the OR&L crossed the Oahu Sugar Company's "main line" into Waikakalua Canyon. Since the sugar company's tracks were there first, OR&L was required to build the crossing and a switch-tender's building, and to observe the priority of OSC trains over those of the OR&L. Victor soon encountered an OR&L train coming downgrade, and he snapped this photograph just as the U.S. Army tank car in the lead passed through the crossing. The identity of the locomotive is unknown, but the flatcars behind it appear to be empty bomb cars.

senger cars arrived for the Army and Navy systems. Some were used exclusively on base, but most of their freight cars were freely interchanged with the OR&L.

Previous books on Hawaii railroads have debated whether or not the Army ever completed an alternate line between Brodie Junction on the northern end of the Wahiawa Branch and Waialua on the North Shore, to be used in emergencies in case the Oahu Railway's main line around Kaena Point was ever blocked or put out of commission by an enemy attack or a natural disaster. According to a Honolulu *Advertiser* newspaper article dated December 24, 1941, that line was in fact built by the Army. It had been started on the 27th of October, six weeks before the War began, and it proceeded at a reasonable rate. However, on the day after the attack on Pearl Harbor, the original company of Army engineers was supplemented by some 250 civilian laborers and their heavy equipment, so that the new line, including a 112 foot long wooden trestle, was finished on the 23rd of December. Fortunately the line

never had to be used by the OR&L, but the urgency with which it was completed shows how critically the railway's linkage between the towns and bases on Oahu was considered.

The end of the OR&L was covered in Volume 1 of this series. The main line was officially abandoned on the last day of 1947. Fortunately the Navy purchased portions of it for hauling ammunition to Pearl Harbor, and a portion remained intact long enough to be placed on the National Register of Historic Places. Thirteen miles of former OR&L right-of-way still exist -- between Ewa, just west of the West Loch of Pearl Harbor, and Nanakuli, on Oahu's Leeward Coast -- and the Hawaiian Railway Society currently runs excursions trains on seven miles of that line, so that residents and tourists can still experience a ride on the OR&L through the Ewa coral plain and northward along a portion of the beautiful coastline. It remain a fine tribute to Benjamin Franklin Dillingham and his railroad.

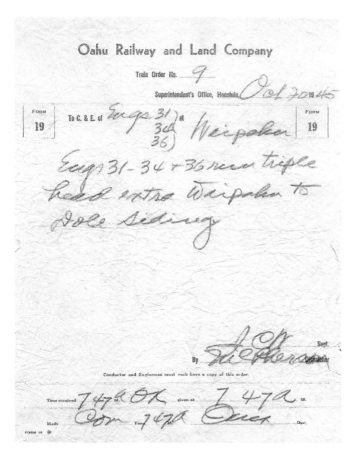

Oahu Railway and Land Company

Train Order No. 9

Superintendent's Office, Honolulu, Oct 30 1945

FORM 19

To C. & E. of Engs 31
34
36 } at Waipahu

FORM 19

Engs 31 - 34 + 36 run triple head extra Waipahu to Dole Siding

By J. A. Hara   Supt.
Dispatcher

Conductor and Engineman must each have a copy of this order.

Time received 747a OK given at 747a M.
Made Con 747a Eng   Opr.

FORM 19

LEFT: This Form 19 train order from Victor's collection shows the lineup for one of the many triple-headers used on OR&L's rugged Wahiawa Branch.

BELOW: Victor walked further up the canyon and observed the parallel rights-of-way of the Oahu Railway and the Oahu Sugar Company. OSC's line is on the left, and it is believed that this is where their line north from the sugar mill split to climb each side of the canyon to reach sugar cane fields at the higher elevations east and west of the canyon. OR&L's Wahiawa Branch, shown here on the extreme east side of the canyon, was obviously built to much higher standards in view of the heavier equipment operating over it. The chimney in the middle background is probably from one of the many pumping stations that provide water from Oahu's aquifer for irrigation of the sugar cane fields.

OPPOSITE ABOVE: Victor returned to the junction at Waipahu in time to catch the Barbers Point extra that he had seen earlier, as it returned to Waipahu on its way back to Honolulu, and he snapped his shutter just as it reached the bridge over Kapakahi Stream, just west of the station. The semaphore signal to the right of #88's smokebox marks the entrance to the Wahiawa Branch, which curves off to the right. Sitting on the line to Wahiawa on the other side of the bridge is U.S. Army tank car #1416, that had just come down the branch.

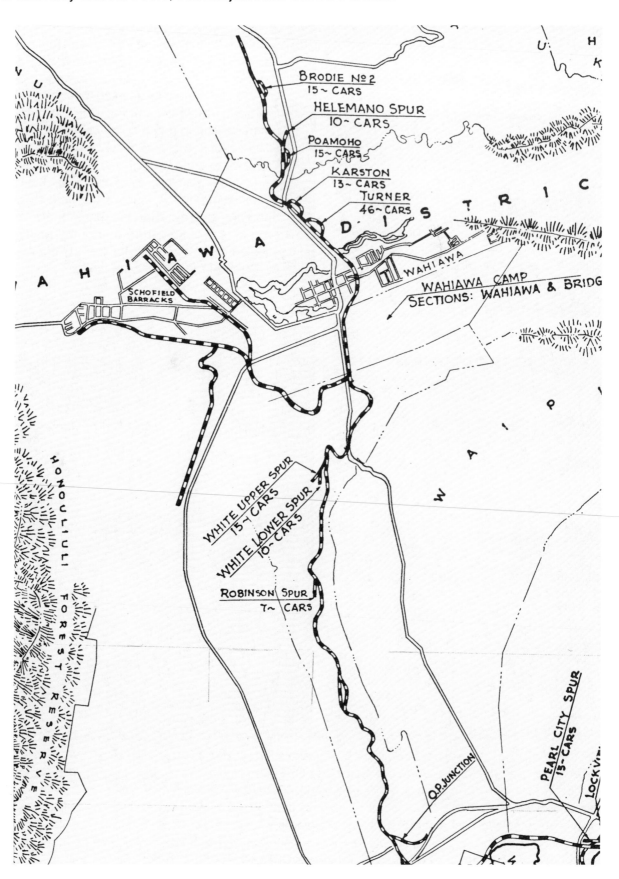

ABOVE: Beyond Waipahu, just west of Pearl Harbor on Oahu's flat coral plain, stood the sugar mill town of Ewa. Ewa Plantation Company was the third sugar plantation along OR&L's main line from Honolulu, and its station, seventeen miles from downtown, was appropriately named Ewa Mill. "Downtown" Ewa, where the plantation offices, railroad roundhouse and mill were located, stood just a few blocks north (to the left) of the little station building shown here. Victor shot this view looking east along the main line towards Pearl Harbor and Honolulu. Ewa Mill Station and this passing siding are long gone, but the main line shown here survives as part of the Hawaiian Railway Society's trackage, although this portion is not currently part of the former OR&L line being used for Sunday operations.

Mormon Temple, Laie

Old King's Highway

Lava Coast, Kaena Point

GREEN—Bus Route
BLACK—Rail Route

Only Complete

SHORE LINE
TOUR OF OAHU
By
BUS and RAIL
SUNDAYS ONLY
OAHU RAILWAY : PHONE 5731

By Bus and Rail

A SHORE LINE TOUR OF OAHU

Itinerary: Comfortable, safe buses of the Oahu Railway leave the entrance of Halekulani Hotel at 8:50 a. m. and the Waikiki Tavern at 9 a. m. and proceed around Diamond Head, through the Kahala residence district, Waialae Golf Club, beautiful Hanauma Bay, to the rocky coast of Koko Head. Here the bus pauses for a short view of the Blow Hole, famous salt water geyser, before swinging into the Makapuu Pass at the old King's Highway.

Over the pass the brilliant blues and greens of the waters, the long stretches of coral sand and black lava rock spread into view. This is windward Oahu, the vacation land of Island residents. At the foot of the pass stand the remains of an ancient Hawaiian village said to be the first landing point of King Kamehameha's warriors. From here the highway leads through Waimanalo Sugar Plantation, past Kaaawa, Kahana Bay, Punaluu to Laie. Laie is famous as the site of the beautiful Mormon Temple. Here a twenty-minute stop is made.

From Laie the route proceeds to Kahuku, a plantation town, and ten miles farther is Waimea Bay, and historic Waimea Valley whose steep cliffs or palis were the ancient burial grounds of the Chiefs of Oahu. The bus trip terminates at Haleiwa, a beautiful spot on the shore of Waialua Bay, where there are several inns that will provide luncheon and innumerable lovely spots to enjoy a picnic.

An hour after arrival at Haleiwa the trip is resumed by rail in comfortable observation cars. Leaving the lush, sub-tropical verdure of the windward side the train swings sharply around Kaena Point and the rugged leeward side of the island sweeps into view. Sharp mountains skirt the shoreline, an-cient lava flows have thrust out to sea, and the sea in turn has carved these molten intrusions into fantastic arches and weird shapes and covered them with jagged growths of coral. Ancient heiaus, Hawaiian fishing villages, one-man plantations of bananas, taro, rice and papaia give a lasting picture of "Old Hawaii." Rolling fields of sugar cane stretch mile after mile and finally give way to miniature rice paddies where water buffaloes plod patiently through the oozing fields enabling the Oriental rice planter to tend his crop by the same picturesque, laborious method that fed his ancestors. Then suddenly the shore line bristles with battleships, and the turrets and buildings of the great Pearl Harbor Naval Station are in view. In a few short minutes, after passing Hickam Flying Field, John Rodgers Airport and the pineapple canneries, the train pulls into the station. It is 3 p. m. and a bus awaits to return you to the Waikiki Tavern.

This is the only complete shoreline trip around the island. Reservations are necessary and may be made at the Halekulani Hotel, the Waikiki Tavern and the Oahu Railway offices.

Leave Halekulani Hotel by Bus . . .	8:50 A.M.
Leave Waikiki Tavern by Bus . . .	9:00 A.M.
(Sunday only)	
Arrive Haleiwa by Bus	11:51 A.M.
(One hour for lunch)	
Leave Haleiwa by Rail	12:55 P.M.
Arrive Honolulu by Rail	3:00 P.M.
Arrive Waikiki Tavern	3:15 P.M.

RATE
PER PERSON $5

Ask for information at
Oahu Railway • Phone 5731
and
Hawaii Tourist Bureau • Phone 6156

TOP: A few months after the end of World War II, OR&L decided to resume its popular railway excursions to Haleiwa via the dramatic Leeward Coast of Oahu. The first of these was scheduled for the 9th of December 1945, and Victor signed up for the trip as soon as he heard about it. Ten-wheeler #88, shown above in Iwilei on an earlier date, was selected to pull this excursion.

ABOVE: The excursion left Honolulu Station at 9:00 a.m. and passed along the pineapple canneries and through Honolulu's industrial area before reaching this median strip where it ran between Kamehameha Highway and Pearl Harbor Road, soon to be renamed Nimitz Highway. Here, just east of Pearl Harbor, the special overtakes a Honolulu Rapid Transit Co. bus on Pearl Harbor Road. Buses like these were Victor's normal transportation between the Navy Base and downtown Honolulu. OR&L's main line was at this time double-tracked from Honolulu only as far as Aiea, on the north side of Pearl Harbor.

OPPOSITE: Here is a pre-War advertisement for an OR&L combination bus and rail tour -- the "only complete shore-line trip around the island."

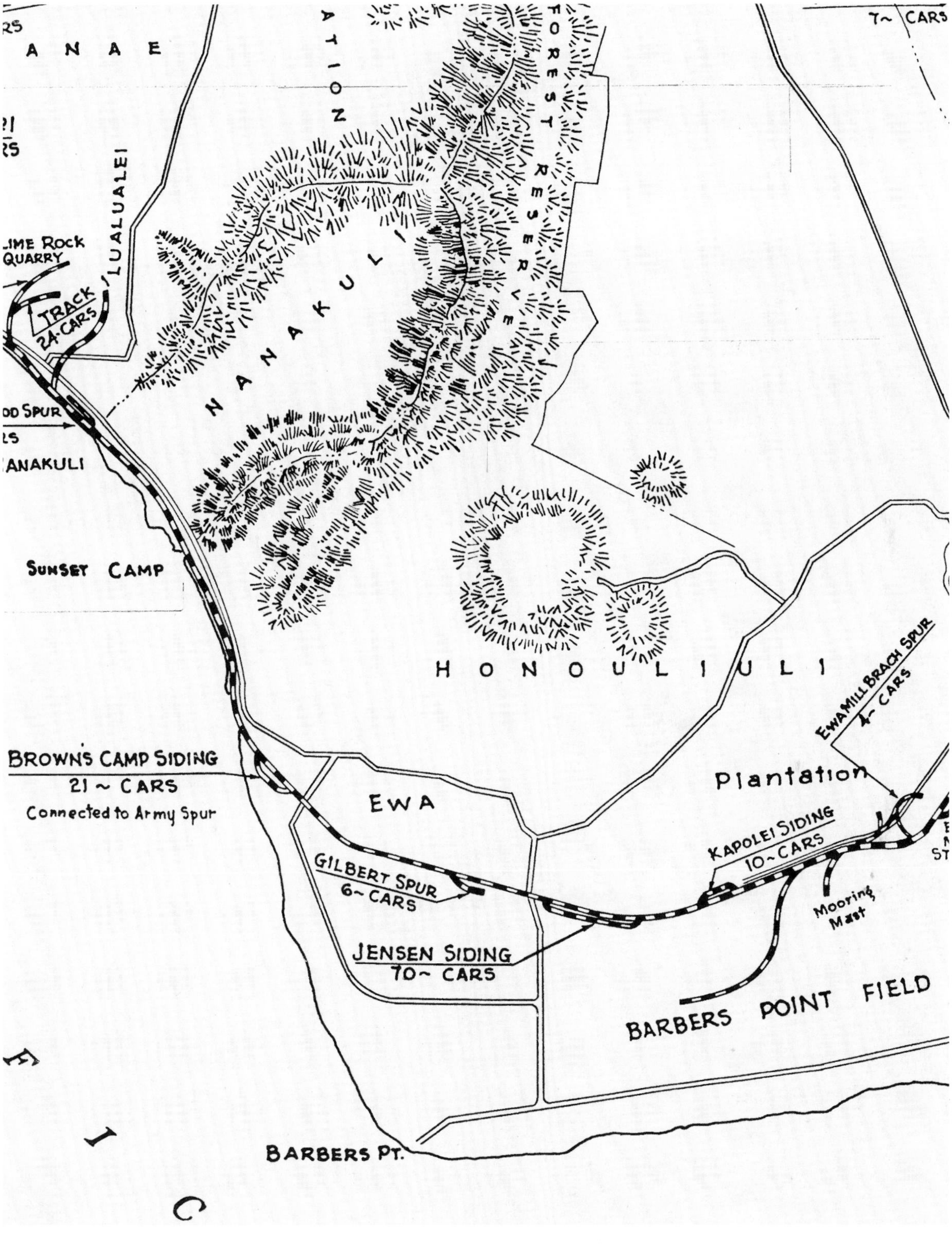
ANAE
LIME ROCK QUARRY
LUALUALEI
TRACK 24-CARS
NANAKULI
FOREST RESERVE
OD SPUR
ANAKULI
SUNSET CAMP
HONOULIULI
BROWN'S CAMP SIDING
21 ~ CARS
Connected to Army Spur
EWA
Plantation
EWA MILL BRACH SPUR
4~ CARS
GILBERT SPUR
6~ CARS
KAPOLEI SIDING
10~ CARS
Mooring Mast
JENSEN SIDING
70~ CARS
BARBERS POINT FIELD
BARBERS PT.
7~ CARS

OPPOSITE ABOVE: Shortly before the excursion train reached Waipahu, it passed the inbound local from Ewa. The location is not 100% certain, but the track on the left is believed to be the eastern entrance into the yard at Waipahu, since OR&L's booklet titled "Station Designations and Mileages" indicates that the main line was double-tracked from Waipio to the Waipahu Marshalling Yard entrance, a distance of about 0.6 miles.

OPPOSITE BELOW: The excursion's first stop for water was at Waipahu, and from Victor's photograph, it appears that many riders took the opportunity to hop off for one reason or another. Once the engineer blew the whistle and the conductor yelled "All Aboard!" everyone who had disembarked scrambled to return to the train. The excursion cars are sitting on the westbound main, and the siding on the right is the beginning of the eastbound main. The third track, behind the train, was actually the beginning of the Wahiawa Branch, as can be seen in the series of Victor's photos taken earlier at the Waipahu Depot.

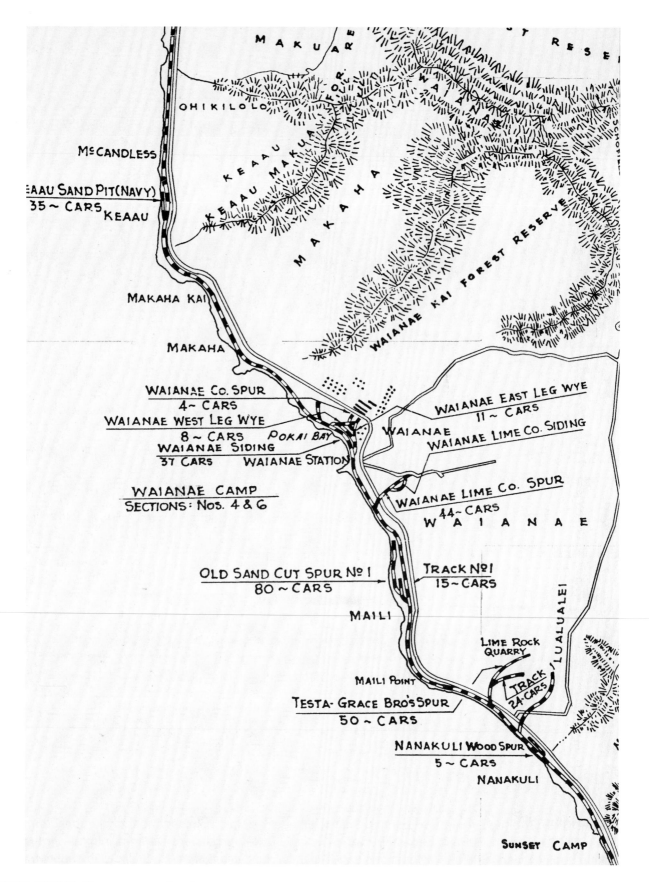

MAKUA

RESE

OHIKILOLO

McCANDLESS

EAAU SAND PIT (NAVY)
35 ~ CARS
KEAAU

KEAAU
KEAAU MAKUA FOR

MAKUA

MAKAHA

WAIANAE KAI FOREST RESERVE

SCHOFI

MAKAHA KAI

MAKAHA

WAIANAE Co. SPUR
4 ~ CARS
WAIANAE WEST LEG WYE
8 ~ CARS
WAIANAE SIDING
37 CARS

POKAI BAY

WAIANAE STATION

WAIANAE EAST LEG WYE
11 ~ CARS
WAIANAE LIME CO. SIDING

WAIANAE

WAIANAE CAMP
SECTIONS: Nos. 4 & 6

WAIANAE LIME Co. SPUR
44 ~ CARS

W A I A N A E

OLD SAND CUT SPUR No.1
80 ~ CARS

TRACK No.1
15 ~ CARS

LUALUALEI

MAILI

LIME ROCK
QUARRY

TRACK
24 CARS

MAILI POINT

TESTA- GRACE BRO'S SPUR
50 ~ CARS

NANAKULI WOOD SPUR
5 ~ CARS
NANAKULI

SUNSET CAMP

OPPOSITE ABOVE: The next stop for the excursion was mid-way up the Leeward Coast of Oahu at the OR&L's fourth sugar mill town, named Waianae, 32.3 miles from Honolulu. Here Victor, and many others, hopped off to snap a photo of #88 as it again took on water. OR&L's freight and passenger stations are behind the two sailors on the left.

OPPOSITE BELOW: On a previous visit to Waianae to photograph the Waianae Sugar Company's operations, Victor snapped this view of OR&L's passenger and freight stations, looking north. The water tank, seen in the previous view, is nearly hidden in the palm trees on the left. Note the Oahu Railway's truck on the right edge of this photo.

OPPOSITE ABOVE: Sightseers from Oahu Railway's first excursion after the end of WWII disembark for a view of Oahu's rugged Leeward Coast just south of Kaena Point, while railfan photographers concentrate on locomotive #88.

OPPOSITE BELOW: This is what everyone had come to see - the rugged, otherwise inaccessible Leeward Coast. The excursion stopped at a point called Arch Rock, just south of Kaena Point, and almost everyone got off to enjoy the view. One wonders if, in today's litigious society, OR&L would have allowed its riders to disembark and climb on the rocks along their right-of-way, risking life and limb? Oh, for the good old days when we were each responsible for our own actions...

RIGHT: This view of #88 and the excursion train was partially damaged by light leaks in the bellows on Victor's camera, but it is such a beautifully composed shot, that it is being included in spite of its flaws.

BELOW: Victor must have been the last rider to get back on board. His friend and traveling companion, Bob Marquet from Pottstown, Pennsylvania, waves as Victor takes his last photo at Arch Rock.

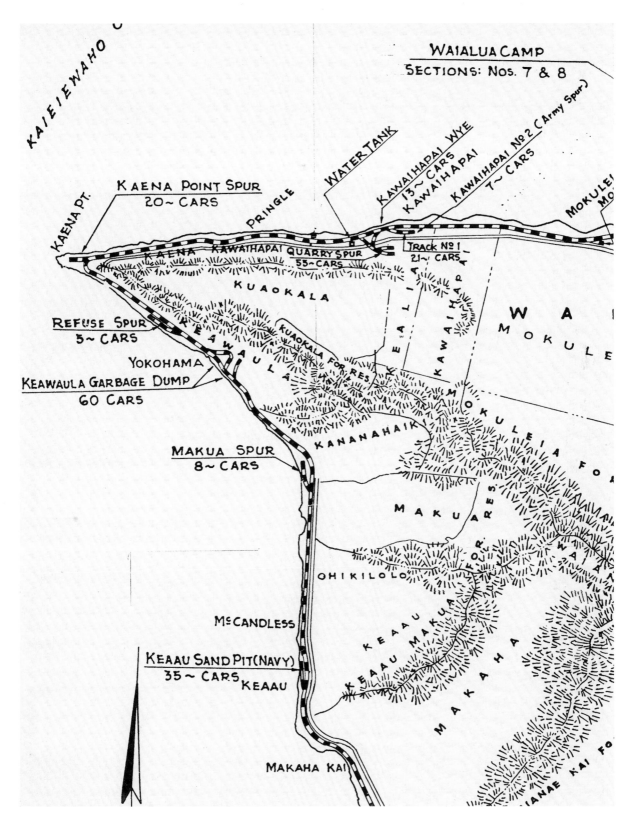

OPPOSITE ABOVE: As the train headed north to the sharp curve at Kaena Point, Victor took this shot over the tender deck and into the locomotive. OR&L's steam locomotives all burned oil, so the decks of their tenders were quite plain except for the two hatches for the oil and water bunkers. Because of that they served as a handy storage area for tools and the re-railers shown here on the left.

OPPOSITE BELOW: Although the ocean looked quite peaceful in the previous photographs, even the small swells seen in the background here can make an impressive show as they break upon the volcanic rocks along the coast. The Pacific Ocean must have put on quite a show along here when the big waves from the winter storms hit this area. Victor titled this view as "Near Kaena Point", and it must have been taken just south of the 19 degree curve where the OR&L turned sharply from a northwesterly to an easterly heading.

Oahu Had A 'Burma Road' Too

Kaena Point has always been one of Oahu's scenic spots which could be reached only by rail—in the minds of the general public, but "now it can be told." During the war it was possible to drive around Kaena Point, not on a super highway perhaps, but still, authorized vehicles did travel the road every day. Here's how it all came about.

Shortly after the "blitz," Army authorities came to see OR&L officials to explain that the defense plans of the island needed a road around Kaena Point, and because of the steep cliff walls and rocky terrain, the only speedy way such a road could be put in was to use the railroad roadbed. The plan was to enter the roadbed at the end of the territorial highway near Makua, continue a distance of 4.1 miles around Kaena Point and leave the railroad shortly beyond, where the Army Engineers had extended and improved the road from Mokuleia.

Realizing that this would create traffic hazards, but recognizing the military necessity for such a road, company officials agreed, and Army Engineers working with the OR&L Construction Gang began operations. The roadbed was covered with coral rock and flooring was placed on the bridges and soon a single track highway was ready for use. Control gates were placed at each end of the road manned by Army personnel and clearance had to be obtained by both trains and vehicles before entering this stretch of road. Even with such an arrangement many accidents occurred, and because of the hazards some one aptly dubbed this section the "Burma Road," a name which stuck for the duration.

Now the Section Gangs are again at work restoring the roadbed to its original condition. New ties have been laid, for covering the ties with rock caused rapid deterioration.

The men of Section 6 and Section 7 were responsible for the maintenance of this portion of the road and they are pictured on the opposite page. Section 6 is pausing in its labors to glance through a new issue of Lanakila, and Section 7—no, they are not having a picnic, it's lunch time and they have picked a nice shady spot under the ironwood trees. Do you recognize the spot? It borders the right-of-way near Mokuleia.

Section 7 —
H. Kunihiro
M. Honda
S. Saito
K. Nakamura
K. Usui
S. Iwamoto
M. Matsumoto

Section 6 —
T. Iwanaka
I. Nishida
M. Otsu
T. Sugiyama
S. Sadamaru
T. Iwahori

This article appeared in the Fourth Quarter, 1945 issue of the *Lanakila*, OR&L's employee magazine. The name Lanakila in Hawaiian translates as "A Victorious Driving Force," which is certainly how many of those familiar with the line's operations during the War would have considered its contributions to our Nation's war effort.

Engine "90" Rounds "Burma Road" Curve

OPPOSITE: After the War, when security lessened, the Fourth Quarter, 1945 issue of the *Lanakila*, OR&L's employee magazine, described Oahu's "Burma Road," shown in the photograph above. An Army post had been established near Kaena Point right after the War began. Accessible only by rail or over the Waianae Mountain range, the OR&L agreed to modify their right-of-way along the rugged Waianae Coast by widening and filling it with coral ballast up to the top of the rails, as well as decking over bridges, so trucks and jeeps could take the shorter trip to their post. There were dispatch points at each end of the dual use portion, and military vehicles were required to call for clearance before opening the gate and driving on the single track right-of-way. The *Lanakila* acknowledged that there had been many accidents along this stretch of track, hence the name "Burma Road." In Victor's photograph album, he titled the above photograph as "End of the Road -- Makua," which is south of Keana Point. Victor's picture of the right-of-way below was damaged during processing, but it clearly shows OR&L's line shortly after the extra layer of ballast had been removed. Of interest to railfans is OR&L's use of standard gauge ties. Once one side of the tie became worn, it could be slid to the far position and used a second time before replacing it.

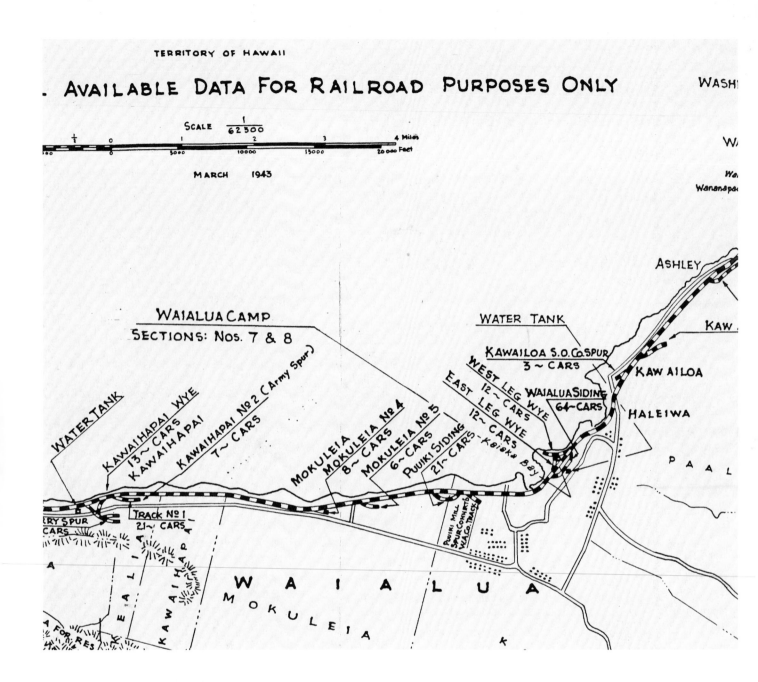

AVAILABLE DATA FOR RAILROAD PURPOSES ONLY

WASH

SCALE $\frac{1}{62500}$

MARCH 1943

WAIALUA CAMP
SECTIONS: Nos. 7 & 8

WATER TANK

KAWAILOA S.O. Co. SPUR
3 ~ CARS

WEST LEG WYE
12 ~ CARS

EAST LEG WYE
12 ~ CARS

WAIALUA SIDING
64 ~ CARS

ASHLEY

KAW

KAWAILOA

HALEIWA

PAAL

WATER TANK

KAWAIHAPAI WYE
13 ~ CARS
KAWAIHAPAI

KAWAIHAPAI Nº 2 (Army Spur)
7 ~ CARS

MOKULEIA Nº 4
8 ~ CARS

MOKULEIA Nº 5
6 ~ CARS

PUUIKI SIDING
21 ~ CARS - Kaiaka Bay

TRACK Nº 1
21 ~ CARS

RY SPUR
CARS

Puuiki Mill
Spur connects
w/ wago track

W A I A L U A
MOKULEIA

MOKULEIA

A FOR RES

OPPOSITE ABOVE: The destination of these postwar Sunday excursions was the small North Shore town of Haleiwa, an early tourist destination created by OR&L building their Haleiwa Hotel here in 1899. Now that the riders of today's excursion have disembarked and are searching for a place to eat lunch, engineer August DeFreitas looks back for the signal from the conductor to back his train to the wye at Waialua, the fifth sugar mill town along the OR&L. There the train will be left on the main line, while the locomotive and the attached combine cut off and run into and out of the short leg of the wye to reverse their direction. The locomotive and combine will then run around the train, back up and couple to what had been the rear of the train. After the air brakes are tested, it will back all the cars to this location, where it will wait for its return trip to Honolulu.

OPPOSITE BELOW: After having been turned and then taking on water in Waialua, #88 returned to Haleiwa and sat along Kamehameha Highway across from Waialua Bay, ready for its 3:00 p.m. departure for Honolulu. Hawaiian railways expert Bob Paoa, who provided the details of OR&L's postwar excursions, said that its scheduled arrival there was 5:30 p.m. Note the design of OR&L's whistle post ("WX"), just to the right of #88.

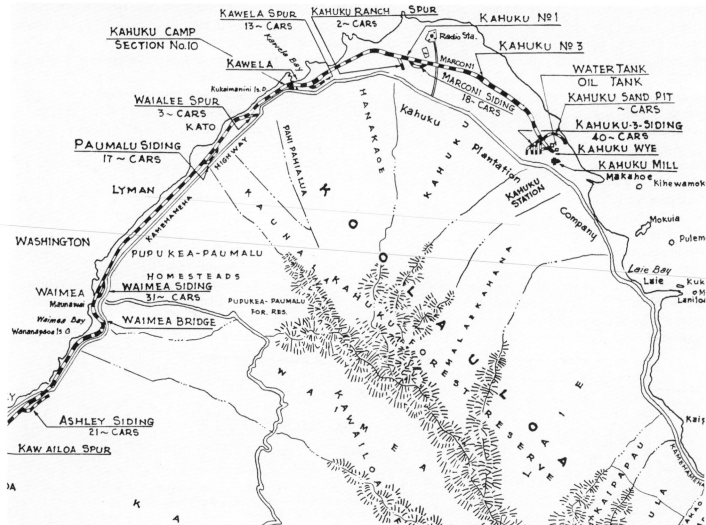

TOP: OR&L's postwar excursions ran every Sunday until abandonment of the main line at the end of December in 1947. Victor caught up with one of the later excursions, again sitting in Haleiwa, with 2-8-0 #22 on the point. The number of coaches in the excursion train determined the size of the locomotive used, with the heavy 2-8-2's being used when the trains reached 15 or more cars.

MEMORIES OF THE OR&L

Since I wrote the first volume, I have met numerous long-time residents of Oahu who have shared their memories of the OR&L. Unfortunately I did not write down their names, but the stories themselves are quite interesting and show how the railroad affected people and their lives here on Oahu. These events were obviously important to them, and although they occurred almost sixty years ago, they are still fresh in their memories today.

Some are simple memories, such as riding a train to the North Shore to visit relatives, or simply for the excursion trip around Kaena Point followed by a picnic at Haleiwa. One lady remembered taking the train with her friends to Camp Erdman for a girl scout camping trip.

A man who grew up in Waianae remembered living right across Farrington Highway from the train tracks. One day his father ordered a new sink for their house, and on the next day the morning freight train for Kahuku made an unscheduled stop right across the street from their house, blew the whistle and then he and has father crossed the street and carried their new sink back home from the train. (From several photos published elsewhere, it appears that the boxcar immediately behind the locomotive that carried the crew also served as an express or less-than-carload freight car to serve individuals and small businesses along the line. In some photographs, this car appears to have a yellow door marking it as a special boxcar with a capacity of only ten tons.)

Another man confessed that he and his brother had often teamed up to raid the pineapple cars as the evening freight from Wahiawa slowed to enter the area next to the canneries. His older brother would climb up on one of the slowly moving cars and pull fresh pineapples from the crates stacked on the flatcars. The younger of the two would peddle his two-wheeler alongside the train and catch the pineapples in his canvas newspaper delivery bag. They would then take the pineapples to Honolulu Station and sell them for a nickel a piece to the sailors returning from liberty. He said the best thing that might happen would be a sailor, perhaps one that had over-imbibed, giving them a whole quarter and telling them to keep the change.

I learned from another man that the OR&L ran a daily roundtrip chartered train for Navy civilian employees, leaving Honolulu at 5:30 a.m. and arriving at the Ammunition Depot at Lualualei in time to start work at 7:30. The train stopped at OR&L stations along the way to pick up civilian employees for Pearl Harbor and Barbers Point and perhaps other military facilities en route. The train laid over at Lualualei and made the reverse trip leaving at 3:00 in the afternoon, returning to Honolulu around 5:00. The gentleman I talked to said he rode it everyday, and they slept or played cards to pass the time. Since it was a chartered train, no tickets were required. Anyone could ride simply by showing his or her government identification card.

One of our Hawaiian Railway Society members, Simon Nasario, wrote and described his memories of the OR&L, just before the War: "From June 1936 to September of 1938, I rode the OR&L from Ewa to Honolulu every day to attend high school. We left Ewa at 6:00 a.m. and got to Honolulu around 8:00. The train stopped and picked up students at Honouliuli, Waipahu, Aeia, Pearl City and Damian Trak, in the area that is now Honolulu International Airport. Also flag stops were made along the way for people who lived too far from the regularly scheduled stops. Fishermen loaded their catches for the fish market in Honolulu, and cannery workers also rode the train. My monthly fare from Ewa was $4.75. The return trip left Honolulu Depot about 3:00 pm. Mail bags and local freight were carried on this run. Along the way bundles of newspapers were dropped off on the fly for the newspaper boys to deliver. There was a bunkhouse at Ewa for the crew, and a wye where the motor coach was turned for the next day's run."

I am sure there are enough stories like those above floating around the Islands to fill a book, but we need to record them now, before the memories fade and colorful events like these are lost forever.

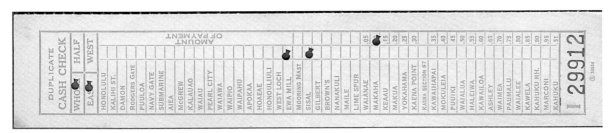

Victor said that he found this fare receipt on one of OR&L's motor cars. In addition to the main stations shown in the OR&L timetable these show all flagstop locations along the main line where passengers could be picked up or dropped off. Concerning the uses of railroad fare receipts, there was an identical half folded behind this one, and after the conductor collected the fare, he punched through both halves the amount, whether full or half fare, direction of travel and the stations traveled between. He then separated the two halves, keeping one half for the railroad and giving the other half to the customer. The travel locations shown here are quite interesting, and the fare seems very reasonable.

HAWAII CONSOLIDATED RAILWAY

ABOVE: Ten-wheeler #99, built by the Baldwin Locomotive Works of Philadelphia in 1900, rests in the yard at Waiakea. This standard gauge locomotive would have looked at home on any American short-line railway. It lasted until the Hawaii Consolidated was abandoned in 1946, and it was finally scrapped in 1947.

OPPOSITE ABOVE: This is the Hawaii Consolidated Railway's schedule effective December 1, 1945. It shows the daily railcar trips over the both the Hamakua (northern) and Puna (southern) Divisions that were running when Victor Norton visited earlier in 1945.

OPPOSITE BELOW: After Victor flew into Hilo Airport in late May of 1945, this was probably his introduction to the Hawaii Consolidated Railway. HCR's passenger station was located on the west side of downtown Hilo, on Kamehameha Avenue between Shipman and Waianuenue Streets, less than 100 yards from the location where the Wailuku River flows into Hilo Bay. The freight station, whose corner is shown on the left edge of the photo, was directly across the tracks. These buildings no longer stand, having been wiped away by the "tsunami" (tidal wave) that struck Hilo on the First of April of 1946.

There were numerous similarities between the Oahu Railway and the Hawaii Consolidated Railway. Like the OR&L, the Hawaii Consolidated -- actually, its predecessor, the Hilo Railroad -- had its origin as a line built to haul raw sugar from a mill to a seaport, where the sugar would be transported elsewhere for refining. It also was founded by Benjamin Franklin Dillingham, although from a financial standpoint it was one of his least successful business ventures.

To truly understand the Hawaii Consolidated Railway, one must first review the geography of the Island of Hawaii, or, as it is referred to locally, the "Big Island." It is the most recently formed island in the Hawaiian Archipelago -- so new in fact that Kilauea Volcano is still flowing into the sea and adding new land to the island's southeastern coast. Hawaii is therefore much more rugged than the older islands that have worn down over the millennia. The northeastern

For the Information and Government of Employees and for the Public

PUNA DIVISION — Time Table No. 27

North 1st Class *2 Mixed Daily A.M. Arr.	Distance from Hilo	STATIONS	Distance from Kamaili	South 1st Class *1 Mixed Daily P.M. Lv.	
8:50	.0	Hilo	33.4	2:00	P. Yards
8:45	1.2	Waiakea	31.2	2:05	P.T.Y.W.F.Yds
8:25	8.3	Olaa	25.1	2:25	P. W. Yards
	13.8	Makuu	19.6		P. Siding
8:00	18.6	Pahoa Junct.	14.8	2:50	P. Y. Siding
7:50	22.8	Pahoa	19.0	3:10	P. Siding
7:30	18.6	Pahoa Junct.	14.8	3:20	P.
7:10	25.1	Kapoho	8.3	3:40	P.Y.W. Yards
6:35	32.1	Kaueleau	1.3	4:10	P. Siding
6:30	33.4	Kamaili	.0	4:15	Siding

(North: A.M. Lv. — South: P.M. Arr.)

HAMAKUA DIVISION — Time Table No. 27

T—TURN-TABLE Y—WYE W—WATER F—FUEL P—PHONE; STATIONS

	NORTH 2nd Class *16 Frt. Daily Ex. Sun. A.M. Lv.	NORTH 2nd Class 14 Frt. Daily Ex. Sun. A.M. Lv.	NORTH 1st Class 10 Mixed Daily A.M. Lv.	Distance from Hilo	STATIONS	Distance from Paauilo	SOUTH 1st Class 11 Mixed Daily P.M. Arr.	SOUTH 2nd Class 15 Frt. Daily Ex. Sun. P.M. Arr.	SOUTH 2nd Class *17 Frt. Daily Ex. Sun. P.M. Arr.
Yards. P.	6:45	6:30	9:15	.0	Hilo	33.7	1:25	3:00	1:00
			9:24	2.5	Paukaa	31.2	1.21		
Yards. P.			9:30	4.0	Papaikou	29.7	1:15		
Spur			9:33	4.6	Paihaaloa	29.1	1:12		
Spur			9:37	6.1	Onomea	27.6	1:08		
Siding			9:40	7.0	Kawainui	26.7	1:05		
Yard P.			9:45	8.4	Pepeekeo	25.3	1:00		
			9:48	9.4	Kaupakuea	24.3	12:5(		
Spur P.			9:54	11.0	Honomu	22.7	12:51		
Yard W.P.			9:57	11.9	Wailea	21.8	12:48		
Yard P.T.	10:30		10:00	12.7	Hakalau	21.0	12:45		11:30
Spur P.			10:10	15.8	Honohina	17.9	12:35		
			10:12	16.5	Waikaumalo	17.2	12:33		
			10:14	17.2	Ninole	16.5	12:31		
			10:17	18.0	Kaiaakea	15.7	12:28		
	P.		10:21	19.1	Maulua North	14.6	12:24		
			10:28	20.4	Kapehu	13.3	12:17		
Yard W.P.			10:32	21.8	Papaaloa	11.9	12:13		
Yard Y.P.			10:36	22.6	Laupahoehoe	11.1	12:09		
Spur			10:46	25.1	Waipunalei	8.6	11:59		
Spur P.			10:55	28.0	Ookala	5.7	11:50		
Siding P.			11:05	31.9	Kukaiau	1.8	11:40		
T.W.F.P.Yds.		9:30	11:10	33.7	Paauilo	.0	11:35	12:00	

(North: A.M. Arr. — South: P.M. Lv. / Noon Lv. / A.M. Lv.)

1—The switch at Olaa Junction will be thrown for the Puna Branch.

2—ON THE OLAA-PUNA DIVISION: All trains North Bound have superior rights over trains of the same class in opposite direction.

3—ON THE HAMAKUA DIVISION: All trains South Bound, have superior rights over trains of the same class in opposite direction. Conductors and Enginemen, Protect your trains (See Rules 45-61.)

*NOTE—a. Trains No. 16 and No. 17 will operate between Hilo and Hakalau only when the Brewer Plantations are harvesting.

b. Trains No. 1, 2, 10 and No. 11 will carry Passengers and Light Freight only. All freight on the Olaa-Puna Division will be handled by extra trains.

BELOW: A few blocks east of the station was Mooheau Park. Here Train #1, the afternoon railbus and trailer combination for Kamaili on the Puna Division, heads east (railroad direction south) along Hilo Bay, past the interesting buses and the single car parked there. The black line along the horizon behind the train is the Hilo Breakwater, built using rocks carried by the Hilo Railroad during the period 1908-1913. Train #1 left Hilo Station at 2:00 p.m. daily, and was scheduled to reach Kamaili, a little over 33 miles away, by 4:15, where it would spend the night. The forward half of the trailer car is filled almost to the ceiling with mail and local freight shipments.

OPPOSITE ABOVE: After arriving on the Big Island, Victor chose one of his first sightseeing events to be a tour of the Hawaii Consolidated Railway facilities in the little village of Waiakea. He walked the mile east from downtown Hilo to the Hawaii Consolidated's operational headquarters, just across the Wailoa River. The first railroad building he encountered was the Waiakea Depot, located at the west end of the throat of the Waiakea freight yard. Just beyond the building the main line split, with the track to the left going to Pier 1, the Kuhio Wharf, where the railroad met ocean going vessels carrying cargo to and from the Hilo area. The track to the right passed through the yard and went on to Olaa, Puna and the branches south of Hilo.

OPPOSITE BELOW: This is the view from the freight yard looking back towards the station and beyond to Hilo. When Victor looked at this photograph some sixty years later, his only comment was, "Just look at that fancy lamp post. No wonder the railroad didn't have any money!"

coast, where most of the rain brought in by the trade-winds falls, is populated every mile or so by a deep gulley, gulch or valley that has been cut into the shear mountains along the coast by runoff from that region's copious rainfall. These cuts range in size from a few feet across to several miles across, and many are in the thousand foot or more range when they reach the coast. For the most part, there is a gently sloping but relatively flat plateau above the coastline where sugar cane could readily be grown, but these fields usually ended at a cliff several hundred feet above the ocean shore, and this plateau was continuously cut by open-

BELOW: This was the heart of the Waiakea facility -- HCR's eight-stall roundhouse and Armstrong (manual) turntable. Waiakea's water tank is on the right, and there is a small yard beyond the roundhouse. This view is looking back towards Hilo.

OPPOSITE ABOVE: This appears to be Victor's first view of HCR's operations. Here we see 2-8-0 #196 shifting cars, preparing the morning freight train for the Hamakua Division. Note the switchmen working the couplers and brake hoses between the cars. Railroading in the old days was difficult and somewhat dangerous work. The tarps covering the cargo on the flatcars are needed for protection from the 200-plus inches of rain that annually falls on this portion of Hawaii.

OPPOSITE BELOW: Here is a better view of #196. This was HCR's only 2-8-0, and also their only locomotive built new by the American Locomotive Company, having been built by Alco's Cooke Works of Patterson, New Jersey in 1916. It had 44-inch drivers and weighed 62 tons. The "whale-back" tender, for hauling the locomotive's fuel oil and water, was the standard type for the Hawaii Consolidated Railway.

ings described above that had been carved by water flowing to the sea. This flat land, abundance of water and proximity to the sea gave this area its great potential for profitable sugar plantations, but transportation costs made this sugar less competitive than that grown on the other islands.

One of the few potential ports for shipping sugar from this area on the east side of the Big Island was Hilo. Located on a flat plain, near sea level, between the mouths of the Wailoa and Wailuku Rivers, it became the principal city on the island of Hawaii as sugar plantations were developed both north and south of it. Those plantations on the Hamakua Coast to the north of Hilo were developed first, shortly after the Kingdom of Hawaii and the United States entered into their Treaty of Reciprocity of 1876, which allowed Hawaiian sugar to enter the United States of America as a duty-free product.

BELOW: Here is another view of HCR's roundhouse, built in 1920 to replace a smaller three-stall wooden version that had been built by predecessor Hilo Railroad. Five locomotives are visible, although only the right four, numbers 121, 3, 196 and 191, can be identified by their number plates. The one on the far left with footboards is presumably 2-6-2 #5. The building survives today as a heavy equipment garage.

OPPOSITE ABOVE: The roundhouse proved to be a busy place, with locomotives running in and out for light repairs or simply a reversal on the turntable. Here 4-6-0 #3 takes her turn on the turntable. The shadow on the cab and tender looks like it was cast by the water tank across the main line from the roundhouse.

OPPOSITE BELOW: In another early morning photograph, Ten-wheeler #99 runs through a shadow of a palm tree as it passes the roundhouse. In the background shop personnel discuss the railbus and trailer that now occupy one of the roundhouse stalls, visible to the left of #99's smokebox.

The land area south of Hilo was broader and would have been easier to develop except that it was heavily forested, primarily with koa and ohia trees. The Waiakea Mill Company was the first sugar plantation in the area south of Hilo -- and, by the way, the first plantation in the Kingdom to use a steam locomotive -- and its raw sugar was barged from the mill, down the Wailoa River, to the unimproved port of Hilo, where it would be carried out in lighters to ships anchored off shore. However, when Mr. Dillingham obtained an interest in adjacent lands that would become the Olaa Sugar Company's plantation, he

immediately envisioned a railway line and quickly applied for a charter, which was granted on March 28, 1899, for his Hilo Railroad. The original eight miles of track were laid to connect the Olaa sugar mill with Waiakea, near what would become the deepwater port of Hilo. This railroad was the only "standard gauge" (with four feet, eight and one-half inches between the rails) common carrier in Hawaii.

As soon as the initial line to Olaa was completed in 1900, a seventeen mile south-easterly extension to the Puna Sugar Company's plantation at Kapoho, near the eastern tip of Hawaii, was begun. From this main line,

BELOW: Here is #196 again, working a string of cars in Waiakea Yard. After the HCR was abandoned, #196 served the Olaa Sugar Company for two more seasons until their plantation transportation system could be converted from trains to trucks.

OPPOSITE ABOVE: Here is a much better view of #99. This light 4-6-0 was built by Baldwin in 1900 as part of predecessor Hilo Railroad Company's first locomotive order, the other locomotive being 0-4-2 saddle-tanker #33. Number 99 had 56-inch drivers and weighed only 43 tons. Both of the original locomotives were at first wood-burners. Later they were converted to burn coal and then finally heavy fuel oil.

OPPOSITE BELOW: Next we see #121, another Baldwin Ten-wheeler, passing through the yard with both the engineer and the switchman, riding on the pilot, checking out Victor and his camera. Unlike the OR&L, HCR used cabooses as seen behind the locomotive. Victor had two light-damaged HCR caboose photos in his collection -- standard side-door caboose #1 shown here, and one side-door caboose converted from a very short passenger coach that looked quite similar to those that served on the Sierra Railway's Angels' Camp Branch.

two almost parallel branches were built in a south-westerly direction to serve additional sugar plantation facilities in the Pahoa and Kamaili districts. Shortly thereafter the main line was extended north into the town of Hilo, and in 1902 another branch, 12.5 miles long, was built from Olaa further inland to Glenwood to carry tourists to the vicinity of Volcano House, already a popular tourist destination adjacent to Kilauea Volcano. It is interesting to note that the Olaa Sugar Co. had trackage rights over much of the Puna Division, and used them to haul cane from their fields to their mill in Olaa as long as the HCR existed.

In 1907 Frank Dillingham and the other owners of the Hilo Railroad and the Olaa Sugar Company lobbied the Territory of Hawaii and the U.S. Congress for a breakwater and other improvements to Hilo Harbor so that large ships could operate there. Their request was granted, but with the stipulation that the Hilo Railroad was to build an extension north from Hilo along the much more rugged north-eastern coast of

ABOVE: Victor's notes identify the location of this photograph as Waiakea Yard, but the background looks like it might be on one of the legs of the wye heading towards Kuhio Wharf. Number 3 was a 4-6-0 built by Baldwin in 1902 as Hilo Railroad's third locomotive. She had 50-inch drivers and weighed 54 tons. Although #3 had received a steam generator and an electric headlight, she kept her original slide valve gear until she was scrapped in 1947.

Hawaii to Honokaa Mill, about fifty miles distant, to bring much needed rail service to the nine sugar mills along the designated route.

There already was a road connecting these plantations, but instead of building expensive bridges to cross the numerous gulches described earlier, the builders of the road had to select from two cheaper but less than satisfactory alternatives -- to either run their road on steep grades down to sea level and back up the other side, or to turn inland and follow the edge of the gulch to almost its end, cross it on a short bridge and then head back along the other side of the gulch to the coast, where the road would resume its original direction. (Plantation railways that had already been built in this area ran parallel to the coastline, much as the Hilo Railroad would do, and they usually selected the latter method when they reached one of these gulches.)

Since such a road was virtually impassible for freight transportation, the sugar mills resorted to various methods to get their raw sugar from the cliffs down to waiting ships. For the most part these included either lowering the bagged sugar on an inclined cable railway to a wharf built on a shallow water inlet and then transshipping the sugar to lighters or small boats that hauled the cargo to ships anchored in deep water; or, lowering the bagged sugar directly to anchored ships via a trolley running down an overhead wire to one of the masts or a tower fixed to the deck of the anchored ship waiting below. Both of these methods were time consuming and quite weather dependent, hence the desire for a railroad line to connect the sugar mills along the coast to the Port of Hilo.

The Hilo Railroad started building its line north from Hilo in 1908, but high construction costs for deep

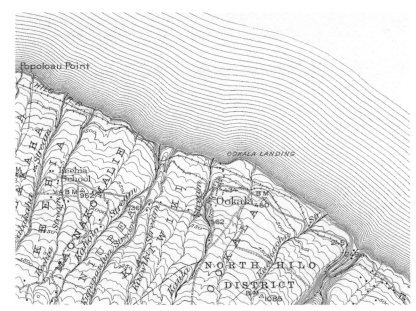

LEFT: The topographical map of the Big Island near Ookala shows examples of the higher standards of construction for the Hilo Railroad (the rail line nearer the coast) versus that of the earlier (and cheaper to build) Kaiwiki Sugar Company. At the upper left the Hilo RR line heads southeast in a relatively straight line, crossing gulches on two high trestles, while the plantation railway runs inland along the sides of the two gulches and then back out to its route paralleling the coast. Just west of Ookala, the Hilo RR also turned inland -- but not as much as the cane railway -- to reach a narrower crossing point. However, on the right side of the map, just east of Ookala, was a gulch that caused the Hilo RR to make a significant detour inland to then require "only" a 485' steel trestle before returning to the coast. (Map courtesy of the University of Hawaii at Manoa)

BELOW: Waiakea Yard, located one mile east of Hilo, was the operational hub of the Hawaii Consolidated Railway. Here were the line's shops, managers' homes, their roundhouse and turntable and a compact yard that begs to be modeled. The leg of the wye at the top of the map went to Kuhio Wharf in Hilo Harbor, the leg to the lower right went south to Olaa and the Puna Division, and the leg to the left went to Hilo and up the Hamakua Coast to Paauilo. This map, based on a Sanborn Insurance map, was first drawn by Hilo railfan, Neil Erickson, then scaled by Ian Birnie and annotated by former HCR employee John May. John Treiber digitized it, and Neil has graciously allowed us to include it in this book. Thanks to all of you!

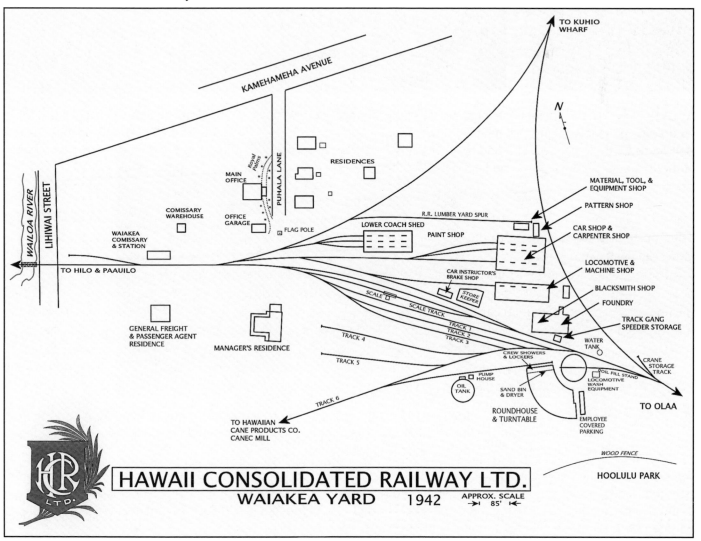

HAWAII CONSOLIDATED RAILWAY LTD.
WAIAKEA YARD   1942   APPROX. SCALE → 85' ←

TOP: This is a beautifully composed shot of #192 sitting opposite the roundhouse, ready to head south on the Puna Division. The conical screen over the flared smokestack caught any sparks that might have caused a blaze during an occasional dry spell. All in all, #192 was a fine looking locomotive.

ABOVE: Here is the right-side view of #192. She is another Baldwin Ten-wheeler, this one built in 1912. (For the most part, the Hilo Railroad, and then the HCR, numbered their locomotives by taking the build year and then deleting one of the digits.) Number 192, like numbers 108 and 191, had 56-inch drivers, 17x24 inch cylinders and weighed 52 tons. All three were scrapped after abandonment in 1947.

BELOW: Number 192 must have sat in the yard for quite a while, allowing Victor to get several shots, including this rear-3/4 view. The building behind #192 is the railroad's backshop, where heavy repairs to locomotives were performed. Like the OR&L, HCR had to be self-sufficient in keeping its equipment operating. Help and parts from the manufacturers were a long way away!

BOTTOM: Here's one more shot of #192, looking back towards Hilo, and showing some interesting cars in storage in the yard behind the roundhouse. Victor had a lot of problems on this outing with light entering his filmpacks -- most likely when they were opened for development. We have decided to repair them as much as possible and use them anyway because of the rarity of the subject matter. We hope you agree.

OPPOSITE ABOVE: These cars were called "bagasse cars." Bagasse is the by-product of the crushing and juice extraction of the sugar cane stalks. When dry, bagasse is somewhat flammable, so it was quite often used to fire the steam plants in the sugar mills and it was even used for fuel for the early plantation locomotives. Eventually it found other uses, including the primary ingredient for certain ceiling tiles and fiberboard, and the HCR had one ceiling tile manufacturer, Hilo's Hawaiian Cane Products, as an on-line customer. Bagasse is bulky but relatively light-weight, so after HCR's passenger traffic dropped to the point where it could be handled by the line's three railbuses, the passenger cars had their clerestory roofs and end platforms removed and windows boarded over on the inside, so that they essentially became large gondola cars. They served the same function as the conventional bagasse cars seen parked with them in the photograph. However, while the latter could conceivably be unloaded (or at least swept out) using the side doors along the bottom, the ex-coaches were not so equipped. It is therefore presumed that both types were unloaded through their open tops using big claws similar to those used for loading and unloading stalks from plantation cane cars.

OPPOSITE BELOW: In Hilo, Victor caught up with locomotive #121 just as her engineer was climbing down from the cab. The 121 was built by Baldwin in 1921, had 50" drivers and weighed 54 tons. It was HCR's last new locomotive.

ABOVE: Victor was fortunate indeed to have ridden over HCR's Hamakua Division, truly one of the world's greatest railway journeys ever. This is train #10, ready for its northbound departure from Hilo Station, with today's consist of Railbus #3 and Trailer #2. It looks like the train already has a nice load for the two-hour trip up the coast to Paauilo, 33.7 miles away. The pair had entered the station less that a half hour before as train #2, the northbound run from Kamaili, having made its scheduled half-hour diversion up the Pahoa Branch before continuing on to Hilo. Light freight and passengers would be exchanged in Hilo before continuing north.

cuts and fills, numerous culverts and small bridges, twenty-two large wooden trestles, thirteen very large steel trestles (all but one over 100 feet high and one 1,006 feet long), plus three tunnels -- one 2700 feet long -- soon brought the railroad to the brink of bankruptcy. The Hamakua Division, as it was called, finally reached the mill at Paauilo, 33.5 miles from Hilo, in March of 1913, but that turned out to be the end of the line. Benjamin F. Dillingham's Hilo Railroad went into receivership in April of 1914, and it was sold in foreclosure proceedings on March 1, 1916.

The reorganized railroad was renamed the Hawaii Consolidated Railway. Few would argue that the HCR's Hamakua Division was one of the most spectacular railways ever built. It was also one of the most expensive, costing $3.5 million, or over $106,000 per

BELOW: Not even 100 yards after departing Hilo Station, the little railbus would rumble over this three-span truss bridge over the mouth of the Wailuku River at its entrance to Hilo Bay. This bridge was one of several that were heavily damaged by the tsunami on April 1, 1946, with the bridge section closest to the camera washed several hundred feet up the river, isolating the Hamakua Division from the southern half of the system.

OPPOSITE ABOVE: Victor managed to get a seat on the ocean side of the train, and his photographs show the ruggedness of the Hamakua Coast. The railway climbed from Hilo to reach the relatively flat area on the bluffs, several hundred feet above the coastline. The cliffs were continually broken by gullies, gulches and valleys, which produced spectacular views from both sides of the train. Here Victor looked down over a cane flume to the ocean below. Because of the sloping land and copious rainfall, water flumes were quite common on plantations along the Hamakua Coast. Cut cane would be floated from the fields down these chutes to either a rail transfer point or to the mill. The water would be used in the mill or would be sent on to irrigate the lower fields.

OPPOSITE BELOW: The government road along the coast was built to much lower standards, so it went up and down and in and out while "paralleling" the railroad line. Victor caught the road and the shore-line below between the bents of another cane flume.

mile -- a world record up to that time. (For those interested, a video showing this construction project, using photographs and written records to document the building of this line, was produced in 1998, titled *Trestles, Tunnels & Tsunamis*.) This line immediately became quite popular with tourists, and the railroad ordered additional passenger cars to accommodate them and ran Scenic Express excursions along the

Hamakua Coast whenever a passenger ship docked at Hilo.

In spite of high operating expenses to maintain this line, the Hawaii Consolidated Railway made steady progress paying off its debt, and supported by increased traffic during WWII, was almost debt free by the end of hostilities in the Pacific. However, Mother Nature did not cooperate, and a giant "tsunami" (tidal

RIGHT: These were Hawaii Consolidated's fare receipts for the Hamakua Division, on the left, and the Puna Division, on the right.

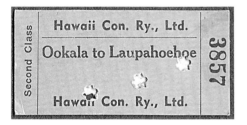

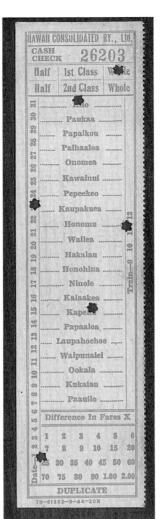

OPPOSITE ABOVE: Victor's photo album labeled this photograph as "Road from Railroad near Laupahoehoe." In this location the railroad was built inland almost one-half mile from the coast, to reach a narrower opening of the gulch, thereby requiring a less expensive bridge. The line also dropped downgrade, crossed the gulch and then went back up again, but it still needed a 130-foot high trestle to cross here. Notice once again how the road has diverted inland as well. With all of these diversions, the distance by road must have been at least twice as far as by rail.

OPPOSITE BELOW: This was the terminus of the Hamakua Division -- the sugar mill town of Paauilo. It might have remained in relative obscurity except that during World War II, the U.S. Marine Corps established an advanced training base, Camp Tarawa, some twenty miles inland near Waimea, and the Hawaii Consolidated Railway at Paauilo was its closest transportation connection. The HCR carried trainloads of Marines from Hilo to Paauilo and return in open gondola or flatcars with benches. It's hard to believe that they would have been as impressed with their journeys as Victor was with his.

wave) hit the Hilo area early on the morning of April 1, 1946. Several bridges on the Hamakua Division were washed away, and the HCR filed for abandonment shortly thereafter. Permission to abandon the line was formally granted by the Interstate Commerce Commission to become effective on December 31, 1946. An attempt was made to sell the equipment piecemeal, but eventually the entire railroad was sold to the Gilmore Steel & Supply Company for scrapping. Operations over portions of the Puna Division continued a while longer as the Olaa Sugar Co. leased the

southern portion of the railroad and some HCR equipment from Gilmore through the 1948 sugar harvesting season, while it worked to substitute heavy trucks for its rail operations.

Over the years the Hawaii Consolidated Railway and its predecessor Hilo Railroad owned a total of eleven steam locomotives, although only eight were on the roster at the end of World War II. As roads improved and passengers left the railroad in favor of cars and buses, passenger service was reduced, and even the lucrative tourist trains to Glenwood for

OPPOSITE ABOVE: The end of HCR's line terminated at the edge of yet another gulley directly ahead of the turntable. The riders for the return trip to Hilo remained on board as an employee prepares to turn the little train on the Paauilo turntable. Railbus #3 and Trailer #2 had been scheduled to arrive as train #10 at 11:10 a.m., and as soon as their direction was reversed they would become train #11, ready leave at 11:35 to make the 33.7 mile run back to Hilo in one hour and fifty minutes.

OPPOSITE BELOW: Although the four-wheeled trailers were built primarily to haul light freight, the heavy war-time traffic loads made them double as passenger carriers. Here, a second employee joins the first to reverse the little train. HCR boxcars in the background will pick up bags of raw sugar from the Hamakua Mill and carry them to Hilo Harbor for trans-shipment to California for refining.

ABOVE: With the reversal just about complete, we get a good view of Railbus #3. The line's three railbuses were originally built by the White Motor Company and were converted to rail service by the addition of flanged wheels. (Why the steering wheel that clearly shows through the window was left in place is a mystery known only to the HCR shop force....) These railbuses were obviously quite successful and ran until abandonment of the railway. They were powered by a four-cylinder Mack engine, and they had 36" diameter rear wheels and 24" wheels on the lead truck. The bus bodies were 19' 3" long and eight feet wide. They were made of wood, sheathed in steel, and were built on a steel frame.

Kilauea Volcano dried up, and the Glenwood extension was removed in 1932. To reduce the cost of the remaining passenger, mail and express operations during the period between the two world wars, the HCR converted one of its passenger cars into a Hall-Scott gasoline powered motor car, which was unsuccessful, and then converted three White Motor Company highway buses to flanged-wheel railbuses. Trailers were added for additional capacity as well as freight and express business. These railcars proved to be quite successful and lasted until the railway was abandoned. A single rail-truck, also for freight and express shipments, rounded out the HCR's motive power roster.

From the Hilo Railroad's beginning in 1899 until

BELOW: For the trip back to Hilo, Victor got a seat at the rear of the trailer and took several photographs from the back of the train. Shortly after leaving Paauilo his train has crossed this trestle near Ookala. By the time the train reaches Hilo, it will have passed over 207 openings under its rails in 33.7 miles, attesting to the ruggedness of the Hamakua Coast.

OPPOSITE ABOVE: The largest bridge on the Hawaii Consolidated was Maulua Trestle, shown here in a view looking north, right after the southbound railbus left the trestle and immediately before it popped into Maulua Tunnel. This trestle was all steel, 1006 feet long, 144 feet high and built on a six degree curve. It was a plate girder bridge with eight towers, and 1103 tons of steel were used in its construction!

OPPOSITE BELOW: Immediately after exiting the 2700 foot Maulua Tunnel, the southbound train passed over another small gulley at milepost 18. It has been said that after leaving Hilo, there were no more than 100 yards of Hamakua Division right-of-way in its original state. The whole railway was a series of cuts and fills, bridges and tunnels. The line was well engineered, with a maximum grade of just 1.4 percent, but it became the most expensive railroad built in the world up to that time, and bankruptcy soon followed its completion to Paauilo.

its end as the Hawaii Consolidated Ry. in 1946, the village of Waiakea, one mile south of Hilo, was the operational heart of the railroad. There the railroad's principal freight yard, an eight-stall concrete roundhouse, maintenance shops and the foundry were located.

We are fortunate that Victor was able to visit the Hawaii Consolidated Railway less than a year before it was abandoned and document as much of its rolling stock and buildings as he did, because so very little of it remains today. Almost all of its buildings are gone. Only the concrete roundhouse in Waiakea, now used as a heavy equipment garage, and the division superintendent's house in Laupahoehoe, which has been turned into an excellent railroad museum, still stand. Many of the large cuts and fills on the Hamakua Division are still obvious, and at least two of the old steel trestles remain is use as highway bridges. Here and there a careful observer can find smaller remnants of the railway, but for the most part the Hawaii Consolidated has faded into history. We are indeed indebted to Victor Norton and the other railfan photographers who preserved so much of it for us.

OPPOSITE ABOVE: Back in Hilo a Marine posed for a photograph by the little train before it continued its journey southward on the Puna Division as Train #1. At Kamaili, HCR's southern terminus, the train would be turned and spend the night, returning to Hilo the following morning. As opposed to the "tourists" visiting the Hamakua Coast and Marines coming to Hilo for business or occasionally for liberty, passenger traffic on the Puna Branch was lighter, but the little railcars provided much needed transportation to the county seat, Hilo, for the residents of the small villages it served.

OPPOSITE BELOW: During the rest of his visit to Island of Hawaii, Victor and his friends spent their days visiting numerous tourist spots around the island, including Kilauea Volcano, Hawaii National Park and Black Sand Beach at Kalapana. On one of these excursions he visited the village of Pahoa and found what appears to be a small railbus shed and turntable. The 4.2 mile Pahoa Branch, from Pahoa Junction, on the main line of the Puna Division, to Pahoa, was built shortly after the turn of the Twentieth Century by the Hilo Railroad, in conjunction with the Puna Sugar Company, to serve cane fields in the Pahoa area. Later this branch became the connection to the outside world for a network of three-foot gauge logging lines that fanned out from Pahoa to harvest the mahogany, koa and ohia forests further up the slopes of Mauna Loa.

ABOVE: During Victor's visit to Hawaii, he found and photographed five of HCR's eight locomotives. (Although 0-4-2T #33 was reportedly not scrapped until 1947, no one seemed to have photographed it, and since it was not mentioned in the scrapping offer, it probably was already gone.) As mentioned in Volume 1, after the War ended Victor corresponded with others who had photographed Hawaiian trains, and he either bought or traded photographs with them. This is HCR #5. She started life as an 0-6-0 built by Alco Schenectady in 1899 for the Sierra Railway. The Hilo Railroad purchased her in 1903 and made the conversion to a 2-6-2 road locomotive in their company shops. Number 5 had 50-inch drivers, weighed a little over 54 tons, and lasted until 1947. Gilbert H. Kneiss, Collection of Victor Norton, Jr.

LEFT: Here we see #108, a Ten Wheeler built by Baldwin in 1908, on the turntable at the Waiakea Roundhouse. She had 56-inch driving wheels, weighed 54 tons and was also scrapped in 1947. Unfortunately the identity of the photographer is not known. Collection of Victor Norton, Jr.

BELOW: This is HCR's inspection car, posed on the Waiakea Turntable. It started its life as a 1930 Studebaker, but otherwise its history is unknown. It looks like another home-built project, with little changed except for the flanged wheels and the third headlight. Again we see that the shop left the auto's steering wheel in place, perhaps so that the driver would have something to cling to while going over HCR's high trestles. This photograph, like several others on these three pages, had been published in earlier books about Hawaiian railroads, so for those who have seen any of them previously, we apologize. However, for most readers these will be new and show even more unique views of this interesting railroad. It certainly is too bad that the Hawaii Consolidated Railway did not survive longer, so more of us could have enjoyed it first hand, rather than through the pages of a book. Vitaly V. Uzoff, Collection of Victor Norton, Jr.

BOTTOM: Number 191 was built by Baldwin in 1910 with 56-inch drivers and a weight of 54 tons. Like all those on the roster at the time (other than #196), she lasted until abandonment and was scrapped in 1947. Photo by Vitally V. Uzoff, Collection of Victor Norton, Jr.

TOP: In this pre-war postcard view, we see a railbus with a trailer headed north, just having crossed Hawaii Consolidated's three-span Wailuku River Bridge. Downtown Hilo is on the right and the Hilo Bay waterfront is on the left. HCR's freight station can be seen immediately to the left of the bridge, while directly across the tracks their passenger station stands, hidden behind the railbus. Both images on this page are from the collection of Victor Norton, Jr.

ABOVE: In addition to the three railbuses, HCR also had this freight motor to carry mail and light freight. It was built in the Waiakea shops from Mack Truck components. Here it is being turned on the small, solid deck turntable located at the west (railroad direction north) end of Hilo Station. The seawall beyond the turntable borders on the Wailuku River, just before the river passes under the bridge shown on the postcard above. Photo by Kent W. Cochrane.

HAWAII CONSOLIDATED RAILWAY EQUIPMENT SALE

After the tsunami hit Hilo on the First of April 1946, separating the Hamakua Division and Hilo from the wharf, the Puna Division and the shops, the Hawaii Consolidated Railway was no longer economically viable. Their management immediately petitioned the Interstate Commerce Commission for permission to abandon the railroad and prepared to liquidate its assets. They hired an engineering firm, Robert W. Hunt Company, Engineers of Chicago, to survey the remaining track material, locomotives, rolling stock, equipment and supplies, to be sold either for use on another property or for scrap. The Hawaiian Railway Society was fortunate to receive a copy of this final engineering report, plus the original negatives of the photographed equipment, through a kind donation from Fred Murai.

This report is quite interesting. It gives specific components, dimensions and condition for each of the line's eight remaining locomotives. Number 121, which had been passing along the Hilo waterfront when the tsunami hit, had been returned to Waiakea for evaluation and possible repair. It was in pieces at the time of the inspection, as was 192, which had been undergoing a major rebuilding when the tidal wave hit. Locomotives 5, 99 and 108 were still in service on the Puna Division, where little or no tidal wave damage had occurred. Numbers 3, 191 and 196 had apparently spent most of their time since the tsunami hit sitting silently in the roundhouse, but all of them, plus the railway's Browning crane, were steamed up to check for leaks and operating capability for this report.

Also offered were their two surviving railbuses #1 and 3, two trailers and freight motor #6. Their track inspection car ("towing car"), a 1930 Studebaker on flanged wheels, was advertised for sale, as were six speeders and six section crew push cars.

The report also described the freight car fleet in great detail, including the location of the cars. Most were on the southern portion of the line, but others

BELOW: HCR's Browning locomotive crane was fired up for testing along with the line's locomotives. By this time, though, the travel mechanism had been disconnected so that the crane was no longer self-propelled. The inspection report indicated that the crane's builders plate had been removed, so the build date and original lifting capacity were not known, but that the railroad reported the capacity was "15 tons when blocked." According to the report, the lifting hoist and the boom hoist both worked satisfactorily, as did the slewing mechanism. The safety valve on the 45" diameter vertical boiler lifted satisfactorily at 110 pounds of steam pressure.

TOP: Caboose #2, unlike side-door, cupola caboose #1, survived the April 1st tsunami unscathed and was offered for sale "in serviceable condition." It was 36 feet long, with arch bar trucks and 33-inch wheels. Its history is unknown, but it would be interesting to learn whether it came to the Hilo Railroad new, or if it was purchased later from another railroad as used equipment.

ABOVE: Gondola car #73 was one of four remaining 36' wooden gondola cars. Like hopper #510, the four gondolas, numbered 27, 73, 75 and 87, were used primarily as cinder cars. The report indicated that the stake pockets and other metal parts, including the truss rods, had diminished due to corrosion in Hilo's humid environment.

TOP: Hopper car #510 was a classic wooden hopper car, built with truss rods and a metal gate, "...arranged for spreading cinders at the center of the track." This was the line's only 36' hopper car, the two others being 40' long with, "...wood and steel Rodger ballast car bodies with a 2' wooden extension on the sides and ends."

ABOVE: A total of 83 boxcars made them the most numerous type on the Hawaii Consolidated Railway. All were wooden with truss rods and arch bar trucks, and although they came in two lengths, 34'-10" and 36', all were rated at 40-ton capacity. Number 88 was typical of the shorter boxcars. The report indicates that over half of HCR's boxcar fleet was marooned north of Hilo.

Hawaiian Railway Album

were "marooned" in Hilo, beyond the damaged Wailoa River drawbridge, or scattered over the Hamakua Division north of the destroyed Wailuku River Bridge. HCR's freight equipment, with the exception of a few steel flatcars, was a wooden car fleet, with truss rods and arch bar trucks on most cars. At the time of the inspection, the roster numbered 201 freight cars, including caboose #2. The car types and quantities were: Boxcars (83), flatcars (65), bagasse cars (25), tank cars (16), stock cars (4), gondola cars (4), hopper cars (3), caboose (1).

In spite of all the information that can be gathered from the report, several significant questions concerning equipment mentioned in previous books arise. First, what happened to HCR locomotive #33, their 0-4-2T, built by Baldwin in January 1900, as one of Hilo Railroad's original locomotives? Best mentioned in *Railroads of Hawaii* that it was scrapped in 1947, but it does not appear in this report. Also missing from the report is the third railbus. Numbers 1 and 3 were

offered for sale, but #2 was not mentioned. Finally there is the third caboose. Best indicated that there were two Sierra Railway coach-like models. The conventional caboose, #1, was destroyed by the tidal wave, and #2 was put up for sale, but no mention was made of #3, nor have any photographs of it surfaced. Did it really ever exist? With the company records having been destroyed by the tidal wave, we may never know.

Although Victor Norton probably saw many of these cars, they were too mundane to waste precious film on. Fortunately the negatives from the inspection report survived, and prints of several of their seldom-seen cars are shown here. Apparently only the scrappers were interested in purchasing HCR's antiquated equipment. A small amount of the HCR equipment listed above, as well as a portion of the Puna Division, was leased from the scrapper and used by the Olaa Sugar Company until their rail service ended in November 1948, and then the balance of the Hawaii Consolidated Railway passed into history.

BELOW: The sale offering listed six section crew speeders -- five from Casey Jones of Eau Claire, Wisconsin, and one from Buda of Harvey, Illinois -- all in serviceable condition. This is track speeder #7, most likely gasoline-powered. It was capable of hauling four men and their track maintenance tools while pulling a small trailer for additional material. The items in the background are interesting, including steel flatcar #213 and wooden flatcar #114, plus the gondola and hopper cars shown previously. The big tank held 10,000 barrels of heavy oil for the railroad's locomotives.

Road No.	Type	Builder	Constr. No.	Build Date	Weight	Wheel Diam.	Cyl. & Stroke	Comments
3	4-6-0	Baldwin	20052	Feb 1902	108,000	50	18 x 24	Originally named "Kilauea", Scrapped 1947
5	2-6-2	Alco-Schenectady	5177	Apr 1899	108,700	50	18 x 24	Ex-Sierra Rwy #3, Acquired 1903, Rebuilt from 0-6-0, Scrapped 1947
99	4-6-0	Baldwin	17318	Jan 1900	86,000	56	16 x 24	Originally named "Olaa", Scrapped 1947
108	4-6-0	Baldwin	32895	Aug 1908	104,000	56	17 x 24	Scrapped 1947
121	4-6-0	Baldwin	54897	Jul 1921	108,000	50	18 x 24	Scrapped 1947
191	4-6-0	Baldwin	35433	Oct 1910	104,000	56	17 x 24	Scrapped 1947
192	4-6-0	Baldwin	37785	May 1912	104,000	56	17 x 24	Scrapped 1947
196	2-8-0	Alco-Cooke	56163	Jul 1916	124,000	44	18 x 24	Scrapped 1950

Data from Best's "Railroads of Hawaii"

COLORS ON THE HAWAII CONSOLIDATED RAILWAY DURING WWII

The Hawaiian Railway Society has no color slides or movies of the HCR, so all of the following are based on black and white photographs and notes and memories from railway historians -- particularly Ian Birnie of Hilo, and John May of Lancaster, California, who grew up on the Hawaii Consolidated. John's father was the last Superintendent of HCR's Car Department, and John worked summers for the HCR just prior to WWII.

Steam Locomotives and Tenders: These were painted black except for light graphite smoke and fire boxes. (Per John May, #108, 191 and 192 had blued steel boiler jackets with brass straps.) Cab window frames were painted scarlet red. Numbers on locomotives and tenders and the HCR circle heralds on tenders were painted white. Locomotive number plates were polished brass, and again according to John May, had the following variations: #99 -- all brass; #5 & 196 -- scarlet red background; #3, 108, 121, 191 & 192 -- black background.

Railmotors and Trailers: Bodies of these were a very dark green, similar to today's C&NW locomotive green. Railbuses and trailers had dark brown roofs and gold lettering and heralds, while #6 had black fenders, an aluminum roof and white lettering and heralds. Wheels, trucks and underbodies were all black.

Freight Cars: HCR's wooden cars were painted caboose red with black underbodies and trucks, while their steel cars were a dark graphite color with black underbodies and trucks. Caboose #1 was painted pullman green, while #2 was painted caboose red. Numbering and circular heralds on all freight cars were white, and all closed cars had dark brown roofs. Wooden decks of flatcars were first coated with hot tar and then covered with gray sand from Hilo Bay.

Passenger Cars: All passengers cars had been converted to bagasse cars or scrapped by WWII, but while in passenger service they were painted pullman green with dark brown roofs and gold lettering.

Stations and Company Buildings: These were generally painted caboose red with white trim, except for Hilo's passenger station which was cream with dark brown trim. The roundhouse at Waiakea was natural concrete. Roofs of these buildings were metal and painted a dark graphite or black color.

Service Facilities: Except for Waiakea's enclosed water tank which was painted cream with dark brown trim, HCR's wooden water tanks were not painted and therefore had natural redwood tanks and natural pine supports. The railway's many steel bridges and their heavy fuel tank and turntable at Waiakea were painted a dark graphite color.

Best, Gerald M., *Railroads of Hawaii,* San Marino: Golden West Books, 1978.

Bonnell, Henry F., *Hawaiian Rails of Yesteryear,* Ewa: The Hawaiian Railway Society, 1997.

Cochrane, Kent W. *The Oahu Railway & Land Company,* Trains, Volume 7, No. 5 (March 1947), pp. 26-37.

Conde, Jesse C., *Sugar Trains Pictorial,* Felton: Glenwood Publishers, 1975.

Conde, Jesse C. and Best, Gerald M., *Sugar Trains,* Felton: Glenwood Publishers, 1973

Gossett, J.R., Editor, "Oahu Had A 'Burma Road' Too," *Lanakila,* Volume 1, No. 4 (Fourth Quarter 1945), pp 4-5

Hawaii Consolidated Railway, Limited, Hilo, T.H., Inspection Report: Track Material, Locomotives, Rolling Stock, Equipment, Bridges, August 1, 1946, Chicago: Robert W. Hunt Company, Engineers, 1946

Hungerford, John B., *Hawaiian Railroads,* Reseda: Hungerford Press, 1963.

Mallchok, Judith, *Trestles, Tunnels & Tsunamis* (Video), Evanston: Brella Productions, 1998

"Railway Now Joins Waialua, Wahiawa," *Honolulu Advertiser,* 24 December 1941

Treiber, Gale E., *Hawaiian Railway Album, Vol. 1-The Oahu Ry. and Land Company, Ltd, in Honolulu,* Hanover: The Railroad Press, 2003

Yardley, Paul T., *Millstones and Milestones, The Career of B. F. Dillingham,* Honolulu: The University of Hawaii Press, 1981